D0556326

toward
a solar
civilisation

Omraam Mikhaël Aïvanhov

toward
a solar
civilisation

New translation from the French

2nd edition

Collection Izvor
No. 201

EDITIONS **PROSVETA**

Prosveta S.A. – B.P. 12 – Fréjus, France

ISBN 2-85566-373-3
édition originale : 2-85566-206-0

TABLE OF CONTENTS

EDITOR'S NOTE

The reader is asked to bear in mind that the editors have retained the spoken style of the Master Omraam Mikhaël Aïvanhov in this presentation of the Teaching of the Universal White Brotherhood.

It should also be mentioned that the word 'white' in the name of the Brotherhood is not a discriminatory reference to the colour or race of its members. On the contrary: just as white light is the sum and synthesis of all the other colours, so the Universal White Brotherhood concerns all human beings of every race, nation or creed and invites them to unite in creating a new world of brotherhood and harmony.

1

THE SUN,
INITIATOR OF CIVILIZATION

As soon as the sun gets up he pours forth his light, his warmth and his life and it is that light, warmth and life that encourage men and women to get up, too, and go to work. Some go off to their offices, some to factories or to the fields, others open their shops and stores. The children go off to school and the streets are filled with the sounds of voices and cars. In the evening, when the sun goes down, people close their shops and offices and go home and, before too long it is time for bed! The daily rhythm of human life is patterned on the rhythm of the sun's movements. And it is the sun, too, who is at the origin of all culture and civilization.

People sometimes wonder who was the first person to teach men the arts of writing and agriculture, the use of fire and certain tools. Various names are put forward but, in reality, it was no man but the sun who was at the origin of these discoveries. You will perhaps say that that is all

nonsense! That the sun is not an intelligent being and that he has neither a brain nor a mouth
with which to speak! According to you, then, ig-
norant human beings have a monopoly on intelligence! The one being to whom all life on earth
owes its existence is not intelligent!

And yet, if you just reflect for a moment you
will see that the sun was the first to bring science
to mankind. How? Well, it's very simple. It is
thanks to the light of the sun that we can see objects, shapes, contrasts, colours and distances. It
is thanks to that light that we are able to see
where we are and observe what goes on around
us, to compare and calculate. Without light
science simply cannot exist. What can anyone
see in the dark? Nothing at all.

And now, suppose I ask who introduced religion, someone who prides himself on being quite
a philosopher might say that it was fear: the fear
of human beings confronted with the forces of
nature. Don't you believe it! That theory stems
from a very narrow point of view. In reality it
was the sun who created religion. It was the
warmth of the sun's rays that first gladdened
men's hearts and awoke in them the need to love
and adore. Love cannot exist in the cold. But
give someone warmth and he will begin to feel
happy and to love. That is how religion first began: thanks to warmth. Of course, for many, 're-

ligion' may begin simply as love for another human being or even for an animal : a dog, a cat or a canary! That doesn't matter! It is a beginning! And one day that love will grow and reach out to the Lord God, the Master of the Universe.

And lastly, it is also the sun who was at the origin of all art, simply because he gives life. Life is what causes a being to move, act and express himself and so you have the beginning of dance, song, painting and sculpture. Art begins with life. Look at children : they are always on the move, shouting, and screaming and scribbling. And their shouts are the beginning of music, their scribblings are the beginning of painting, their sand castles are the beginning of sculpture, the little houses they make are the beginning of architecture and all their little gestures and movements are the beginning of dance. Yes indeed! All art begins with life and life comes from the sun.

How could an artist create if the world were plunged in darkness? Where would he find his models? Who would give him the notion of movement, form and colour? I sometimes say to artists, 'You paint pictures, but who gave you the colours? Was it you who made them? No. By means of the various vegetables or minerals concerned it is the sun who has given you those colours. Do you ever think of that?' But it never

seems to occur to painters to thank the sun for
their colours. And, in fact, it is rare that the sun
figures in their works.

So, you see, the sun gives light, warmth and
life and hence he is the father of science, of religion and art. And yet he is the last one to be
loved and respected by human beings. But that
is where I'm different: I'm for the sun! I'm calling for his rehabilitation. It makes me indignant
to see how people treat him: they raise monu-
ments to all kinds of impostors and never to the
sun! And yet he is the first cause, the origin of
everything. The earth itself and the other planets
all come from the sun. It was he who begot
them. That is why the earth contains the same
elements as the sun but in condensed form, as
solids. All the minerals, metals and precious
stones, all the plants, all the gases and all subtle
or dense bodies – whether in the soil, in water, in
the air or on the etheric plane – all come from
the sun. Gold, for example – which human beings appreciate to the point of being ready to
commit all kinds of crimes to obtain it – gold is
formed by the sun. Just as, on the surface of the
earth there are factories that manufacture all
kinds of objects similarly there are factories under the surface of the earth which employ millions of entities, and it is they who condense
sunlight to produce gold.

I can hear you object, 'But how can gold be condensed sunlight?' Let me make it clearer with the example of a tree. Trees, especially oaks, firs, pines and walnut trees, are composed of a very hard, compact material which can be used to build houses and boats, etc. A tree grows out of the soil and hence it has always been presumed that a tree is made of soil. But that is completely untrue. A tree is made of sunlight. Take a tree, as big a tree as you like, and burn it. What will you see? Flames. Quantities of flames, a lesser amount of gases, even less water vapour and, at the end, you will be left with a small, a very small, pile of ash. So much for the soil!

A tree is made of earth, water, air and fire, but it is the fire, the sun's rays which go to make up the major part of its bulk. So, a tree is not made of soil. It's made of condensed sunshine! You only have to visit some of the forests that I have visited in India, Ceylon, The United States, Canada and Sweden, to realize that all those trees, which must weigh billions of tons, have not lowered the level of the ground on which they stand. If they had taken out of the soil all the elements that constitue their bulk the ground should have sunk several hundred feet. This is just one more proof that a tree is made of condensed sunlight. And if trees can collect and so-

lidify the sun's rays in this way, why shouldn't it
be possible for certain entities working underground to do the same and produce gold? Oh
yes, there's a lot of food for thought in all this!

I once knew a man whose over-riding passion
was to find gold. He had all kinds of books about
hidden treasure and the magical practices which
were supposed to help him find it. For quite a
while I left him to it and said nothing (and, of
course, he didn't find anything!). And then, one
day I asked him why he persisted in carrying on
with the chambermaid instead of trying to win
the friendship of the lady of the house. He was
very indignant and declared that he was an honest married man and wasn't carrying on an affair
with anyone. I replied, 'Yes, of course, I know
you're a faithful husband, but I can see that you
are still trying to seduce the maid.'

Of course, he still didn't understand, so I explained, 'You see, you're always looking for
gold. But gold is only the servant. The lady of
the house is the sunlight which, when condensed
in the depths of the earth, becomes gold. And
when the lady of the house sees that instead of
trying to charm her and become her friend you
pursue her maid, she is offended and closes her
door to you. From now on, go straight to the
lady of the house, to the sunlight. Try to love
her, to understand her, to attract all her bless-

ings and favours and some day, sooner or later, you will receive gold. Why not go straight to the top? If you are the king's friend all his subjects will respect you. But if you are a friend of the doorman you'll never get any further than the doorman. No one else will bother with you!' He was astounded. 'I understand,' he said. But I doubt it, because he's still flirting with the chambermaid!

But gold is not the only matter that is a condensation of the light of the sun. Coal, oil, wood and the materials used in manufacturing all kinds of objects are all condensed sunlight. Everything produced by industry, even the clothes we wear, comes from the sun. The whole of our economy is based on the products of the sun, but the sun itself is neglected and forgotten. People forget the creator and run after the outer skin, the peelings, the dross of his creation.

Something is very wrong with men's understanding of these things and it is this error of understanding that is the cause of their greatest misfortunes, for when one abandons the centre in favour of the periphery, when one ignores the essential and pays attention only to what is secondary one is inevitably heading for disaster: and disaster is what occurs. That is why it is high time to restore the sun to his rightful place ahead of every other consideration, for it is he who is the cause of everything. If you do this the situation will improve, first of all in your own minds and subsequently throughout society. Everything will go better. You will ask, 'But how can our attitude towards the sun lead to such fantastic results? It's only a detail.' Of course, it seems a detail, but in the long run the reversal of values which we see in today's world has brought about extremely serious and complicated consequences in all areas of life.

If you reflect for only a minute you will realize that the sun is at the origin of everything. Ask him to explain to you how he meditated and worked so that human beings may live. How did he prepare the right conditions of temperature and climate? How did he calculate just the right amount of light and heat for life to appear on earth? Plant life was the first to exist, followed by fish, birds and mammals and, finally, man. It was the sun who made ready all the conditions necessary for the birth of culture and civilization. Indeed, it was the sun who was the very first farmer since it was he who distributed the various varieties of plant life over the face of the earth and it is he who makes them grow and give flowers and fruit. It is the sun who commands poverty or plenty, famine or abundance.

When I first came to France, in 1937, I remember saying that in the future, men would no longer use wood, coal or oil to produce energy. They would use only the sun's rays. People were a long way from believing me at the time but they are beginning to see that I was right, because it is now well known that the present sources of energy will soon be exhausted and men will be obliged to turn to more subtle sources of energy which are inexhaustible. In the future we shall all draw our light and heat from the sun. We shall travel thanks to the sun's energy. We shall even be nourished by the light of the sun.

Deprived of sunshine men could never have existed. They could never have moved or worked. Without the warmth of the sun they could never have experienced feeling. Without his light they could never have had the faculty of sight, and not only on the physical level but also on the intellectual level: they could never have had understanding, for understanding is a higher form of sight. As for the sun's warmth, well, that is what awoke in man everything that concerns the emotions: contact and exchange with others, love and friendship. It is the sun's warmth that is at the origin of marriage, the family, human society and all forms of community. If you are cold, people don't like you, they leave you alone. But if you are warm-hearted they come and warm themselves at your contact and they are grateful to you for that warmth. Warmth is what draws human beings together. It is what gives them the capacity to feel, to be moved, to wonder and to pray. So you see, the warmth of the sun is at the origin of all morality and religion.

Of course, I know that if you say that to Christians they will be indignant because they don't recognize the importance of the sun. For them, what counts is the Mass. But then I ask them, 'But if the sun weren't there, how could you say Mass? In utter cold and darkness who could say Mass? Where would the bread and wine come from?' I have no wish to belittle the importance of the Mass, in fact I tell you frankly, I know much more about it than most priests. They've learned to say Mass but they know nothing of its deeper, magical significance. I know that. And I have a much deeper respect for Mass than Christians. And yet I still ask them, 'Without the sun, who would say Mass? And who would assist at Mass?' The trouble is they just don't think!

And now, if I tell you that it was the light of the sun acting on our physical bodies that formed our eyes you won't believe me either. And yet it is the strict truth. The sun created our eyes. And why? Well, so that we could see him! In the same way it was his warmth acting on our bodies that created the organs of feeling: the heart, the mouth and, above all, the skin and the sense of touch. He decided that only the eyes should be sensitive to light but that warmth should be felt by the whole surface of the body. You see the difference, don't you? Isn't that interesting?

The sun commands everything in the universe. He is like the conductor of an orchestra or a king on his throne. When he decides something he only has to give the signal and all the spirits he has sent to earth or to the other planets hasten to carry out his wishes. They modify something in the atmosphere or in the electromagnetic currents and all kinds of changes take place in the vegetable, animal and human kingdoms, in the biological, psychological, economic and social spheres. Everything that happens on earth is commanded by the sun. Solar eruptions and sunspots are simply signals that the sun sends out to a whole hierarchy of intelligent beings who are there to carry out his orders.

One day Science will accept my ideas. It is impossible that it should not tread the same path. And that is why, here and now, I say to scientists, 'Leave what you're doing in the laboratories alone and give all your attention to the sun. Everything is in the sun: health, wealth and the happiness of mankind.' You may say that many astronomers and physicists already are studying the sun and, of course, that is so. I know. I am well aware of all the research that is going on in many countries and particularly in Russia and the U.S.A. But when I reproach the scientific world for not giving enough attention to the sun, I mean that they have not yet really studied what the sun's light is and, above all, how man can work with it and let it penetrate him to purify, strengthen and regenerate him. For, if the sun's rays can penetrate even the depths of the oceans so that certain fish specially equipped to do so can capture their energy and give off light, why be surprised that they can also penetrate us? And if we knew how to receive the sun's rays within us they would set in motion certain centres and light certain lamps that have been prepared within us from the beginning of time.

For me, as I have already said, the sun's rays are like so many little wagons filled with food. And this food consists of elements and solar energy to which we can all help ourselves to our heart's content if we want to grow and develop on the physical and psychic levels.

Everything that man needs is contained in the light of the sun. What an immense field for scientific exploration!

2

SURYA YOGA

I

Nowadays, yoga is a popular topic of conversation. I have already spoken to you about it and explained the different kinds of yoga, most of which come from India and Tibet while some come from China and Japan. All religions have their own particular form of yoga – even Christianity. Christians have always practised adoration, prayer, love and veneration of the Creator. These are the characteristics of the Christian religion and in India they are known as Bhakti yoga, the yoga of devotion, adoration and spiritual love. The only problem is that this particular form of yoga suits certain temperaments but not others. Some people have gifts and qualities that call for other modes of expression. The ways that lead to the Creator are innumerable. Christians have restricted themselves to one way, and it is a truly marvellous way; there is no reason to criticize it. But Hinduism is richer in that it has produced many different methods.

For those who have a taste for study, reflection, intellectual activity, they have Jnani yoga, the yoga of knowledge, which is a way to reach God through deep thought. Some people are drawn neither to philosophy nor to mysticism but they have great will-power and energy and dedication. They want to work for and serve others. For them there is Karma yoga, the yoga of good works, of duties to be accomplished with no expectation of reward or payment. Karma yoga is the yoga of gratuitous and disinterested service.

For those who feel the need to control and dominate their own instincts and impulses there is Raja yoga. By means of concentration and self-control they too can reach the Eternal Father and fuse their being with His. The word 'Raja' means 'King', and they become kings of their own inner kingdom.

Kriya yoga is the yoga of light. It consists in thinking of light, in getting to know and understand it, in surrounding oneself with colours, imbibing and projecting colours. It is a magnificent way to work. Kriya yoga is the yoga that Babaji practised.

Hatha yoga is good for those who have a taste for physical exercise and like to assume all kinds of postures or '*âsanas*' as they are called. They fold themselves in two, twist themselves around, roll themselves into a ball, get their legs behind their heads, etc. These exercises, which are of course based on an exact knowledge of the centres which can be activated by the various postures, require a lot of will-power and perserverance. Hatha yoga is the form of yoga best known in the West, but the poor Westerners have neither the temperament and physical constitution of Orientals, nor the calm and silence needed to practise it. The result is that many end by ruining their physical and mental health. How many people have I met who confessed that they had given up Hatha yoga because they felt themselves becoming unbalanced! One should be very prudent about this and I, personally, have never encouraged Westerners to take up this form of yoga.

Agni yoga is the yoga of fire. It consists in thinking of fire, in working with fire, in awakening fire. Since it is fire that is at the origin of all creation, Agni yoga is yet another way to reach the Creator.

Shabda yoga, the yoga of the word, consists in pronouncing certain formulas or '*mantras*' at certain specific moments, a specific number of times and with a specific intensity. The word is a force and someone who knows how to use that force can get significant results.

But now, I want to talk to you about a form of yoga that surpasses all others: the yoga of the sun. In the past this form of yoga has been practised by many peoples and civilizations but in our day it has fallen into disuse, particularly in the West. The Sanscrit word for the sun is '*surya*', which is why I call it Surya yoga and it is my favourite because it combines and sums up all the other forms of yoga. Yes, why not combine all the different kinds of yoga in one?

A disciple of the Universal White Brotherhood cannot be narrow-minded or restrictive. He must grow in all the dimensions of his being. He should act with total disinterestedness: that is Karma yoga. He should seek God and love and adore Him: that is Bhakti yoga. He has to meditate and concentrate in order to achieve mastery of himself and authority over his population of cells: this is Raja yoga. When he is sitting in meditation or doing the movements of our gymnastics or the Paneurhythmics one could say that he is practising Hatha yoga. When he projects light and colour, when he builds a luminous aura around himself, he is practising Kriya yoga. He concentrates on fire and calls on it to consume all impurity within him: that is Agni yoga. He is constantly on guard so as to control every word he utters, so as to avoid saying anything that might introduce doubt or discouragement into someone else's heart and mind. On the contrary, he always tries to become a creator of the new life : that is Shabda yoga. Finally, he concentrates his love and attention on the sun, he tries to maintain contact with it at every moment, he considers it as the open door to Heaven, the manifestation of Christ, God's representative : that is Surya yoga. The disciple who practises Surya yoga rejects none of the other forms, quite the contrary, and as a result he becomes a whole being and lives in inner plenitude.

The portrait I have just drawn for you is a portrait of the coming humanity. In the Universal White Brotherhood, men and women develop all the qualities and virtues, For Surya yoga includes them all : adoration, wisdom, power as well as purity, activity and dedication, light and the sacred fire of Divine love. Now you can see how important it is that you realize what great blessings you receive when you go to see the sun rise in the morning.

By the practise of Surya yoga you establish a link between yourself and the power that governs and gives life to the whole Universe : the sun. That is why you must necessarily get results ! That is why I can assure you that all these different kinds of yoga that were considered so

wonderful in the past – and which still are wonderful – will, one day, be replaced by Surya yoga
which surpasses every one of them for, through
the sun, we work with God Himself. I can even
say that certain things which no human being
could ever teach me have been revealed to me by
the sun. No book can give you what the sun
gives you if you learn to have the proper relationship with him. Up to now you have not
learned to establish real contact with the sun. He
is there, before your eyes, but you do not really
relate to him. You are content to observe that
he's there and that he's a little brighter, or less
bright, than the day before. But that is not the
way to establish rapport with the sun. If you
want to create a bond between yourself and the
sun, when you look at him you must be fully
conscious of what you are doing. Only then will
there be a communication of vibrations between
the sun and you in which forms and colours, a
whole new world, will be born. And this conversation between the sun and yourself will attract
forces and intelligent beings of the invisible
world who will come to dance and steep themselves in the beauty of this dialogue. Of course, I
know that it is not easy to achieve this. If you
really want to obtain all these blessings from the
sun you have to prepare yourselves. And what
does that mean, exactly: to prepare oneself?

Well, let us suppose that you decide to go and
see the sun rise but that the day before, or even a
couple of days before, you have lived in a climate of passions and quarrels. Obviously, you're
not prepared! While the sun is rising you will be
besieged by the memory of your chaotic experi-
ences. Even though the sun is there and you are
basking in his light you will have no feeling of
his presence.

So, you should get ready the day before: try
not to eat too much, not to get to bed too late.
Don't do anything that might torment or worry
you next day. Try to arrange things so as to be
free, your mind clear and your heart at peace,
with no loose ends to be tied up and nothing to
regret or repair. This is very important! Then,
in peace you can begin, slowly and gently, to
meditate without trying to concentrate all at
once on the sun. First of all, take a look at your
own 'inhabitants' and if there is some noise and
commotion amongst them try to pacify and re-
concile them. For it is only when you have managed to free yourself, only when peace and harmony reign within you, that you can project
yourself outward, to the sun. Then you can picture it as a wondrous world peopled with the
most perfect creatures, beings of light who live
in sublime intelligence and in absolute love and
purity. Think that in that glorious world reigns

an order, a culture and a civilization that surpass all imagination!

And now, suppose I told you that, although you don't realize it, you are already in the sun? You don't feel it, but a very small particle of you, a very, very subtle element of yourself lives in the sun. Science has not yet begun to study man as he really is. It has no idea of the immensity, the riches, the depth and the magnitude of man. That which we can see with our eyes, the visible body, is not man. Man possesses other bodies (astral, mental, causal, buddhic and atmic) which are composed of progressively more subtle matter.

But what is true for man is equally true for the earth. The earth is not just the physical reality that we can see and touch. Surrounding the earth is an atmosphere over two hundred miles deep which science has divided into several different layers, each with its own name. But what science does not know is that in each layer there is an infinite number of elements and entities, and that beyond the atmosphere known to science, lies the earth's etheric body which extends as far as the sun, which actually touches the sun. So, you see, the earth's etheric body fuses into the sun's, for the sun, also, has an etheric body which reaches far beyond his own sphere, to the earth and beyond, to all the other planets. And that is how the sun and the earth can actually touch each other. They are already fused together.

And since man is built on the same pattern as the Universe, he too possesses a subtle body which is linked with the sun. This is why, considering the higher, divine dimension of man, we can say that he already dwells in the sun. He doesn't realize it, of course, because his consciousness is still restricted to the visible world.

What I have just said will seem unbelievable to you, no doubt. And yet, believe me, these are truths which you should know and try to fathom. Once someone begins to study in the divine school of the Universal White Brotherhood he begins, gradually, to move from the narrow limits of a strictly sensorial and physical consciousness to the higher, vaster realms of the superconscious. The realm of the superconscious is immense and contains thousands of different levels which all have to be scaled before one can feel that one is truly a citizen of the sun, that one already exists in the sun.

That part of ourselves, that entity which lives in the sun is our Higher Self. Our Higher Self doesn't dwell in our physical body. If it did it would constantly accomplish prodigies! From time to time it comes to visit the brain, but as our brains are not yet ready to synchronize with

it – in fact they cannot even bear its vibrations
–the Higher Self is unable to manifest itself.
However, it continues to work on the brain, preparing it. And as soon as the brain is capable of
receiving it, the Higher Self will come to dwell
permanently in man.

Our Higher Self is none other than God. A
part of God. That is why, on the highest level,
we are God Himself, for apart from God there is
nothing. God manifests Himself through creation and through each one of His creatures and
we are, therefore, tiny particles of Him. We have
no existence apart from Him. The real illusion is
to believe that we are separate from God. When
the sages speak of maya, illusion, they are not
speaking of the material world. The world is not
a maya. It is our lower self that is the maya because it gives us the impression that we exist as
beings separate from the Divinity. The world is
a reality. So is matter. I repeat: the illusion
comes from our lower self which insists on making us feel that we are separate beings.

As long as we continue to live on this inferior
level, on the level of our lower self, we shall continue to live in error and illusion and we shall
never experience that unique and universal life,
that cosmic Being who fills all of space. Our
lower self prevents us from feeling and understanding that Being. And that is why the work

we do at sunrise, through our prayer and meditation, is aimed at renewing the contact, building a bridge between our lower self and our Higher Self which lives in the sun.

As long as you continue to be influenced by mechanist philosophy which would have you believe that the sun is incapable of speaking to you and helping you, you will bar the way to your own evolution. You must understand that everything is alive; that a living intelligence manifests itself through everything we see; that the sun is an intelligence, a life, a living light. And when you understand that, all of a sudden he begins to speak to you. If he has already revealed so many things to me it is because I see him exactly as he is: a spirit of such extraordinary loftiness, beauty, grandeur, power and intelligence that all else pales in comparison! Just try! Try asking him questions and you will see that he will answer you. Perhaps you won't be able to understand his answers at once, but sooner or later they will show up on the screen of your mind. The sun's replies are given in a flash, like an electronic machine. It is up to human beings to grow and develop sufficiently to be able to understand them at once.

II

Several decades ago, as we all know, Science discovered that space was filled with waves. It was this discovery that led to the invention of the radio, telephone, radar, etc... the problem being simply to build machines that could send and receive waves.

But why should science and technology be the only disciplines to exploit this discovery? Space is filled with waves. True, but not only the kind of waves that enable us to make phone calls or to tune in to a programme on radio or television. There are other, much more subtle, waves travelling through space and we must learn to tune in to them. We have the means to do so. God has placed in man all the equipment he needs to tune in to the waves sent out by the sun, the stars and by all the highly evolved creatures which people every region of space. But instead of receiving their messages, instead of switching his receivers to their sublime wavelengths and

drawing from them everything he needs to improve both his physical health and his grasp of
reality, man is forever running after other things.
He is tuned in to other, diabolical transmitters
which fill him with the sounds of strife and revolt. The only thing to do is to learn to tune in
to other stations. And you can do that at sunrise.
Every morning, when you come to the Rocher*,
try to bear in mind that you can receive the
waves that come from the sun. Instead of continually brooding on your grievances and your un-
solved problems, think that you can tune in to a
heavenly transmitter. If you don't do this you
will always be the same poor, unhappy soul who
cannot see what he can possibly get out of going
to see the sun rise!

In fact, of course, I know very well that some
of you say, 'Why go up to the Rocher every
morning? I don't get anything out of it.' The
point is that everything depends on the way you
look at it. If the grumblers had the honesty to
admit that their lives were one mass of problems
and difficulties and that they could see no way
out, and if they went to the sunrise and laid out
all their problems before the sun so as to find the
solutions, perhaps, in point of fact, they would

* The 'Rocher' is the rock at the top of the hill which the
disciples climb to watch the sunrise at the Bonfin.

find the answers they are looking for. Well, why not? In the morning, in the light of the rising sun, take a good look at all your difficulties and the sun, who can see you, too, will say, 'There's an unhappy fellow. Let's enlighten him. Let's help him.' And how, you may ask, can the sun help? By the light waves he sends out.

No one has the right to lay down the law about anything whatever if his consciousness has not yet been awakened. If he does, he will inevitably be wrong. That is why I have repeated thousands of times already that, in order to be present at the sunrise in the correct way, you must prepare yourselves the day before. You must entertain only the best thoughts and feelings before falling asleep. In this way you clear the ground during the night and you can arrive at the sunrise fully awake and in good form, with the thought, 'The heavens are speaking to us. The angels are speaking to us. They are sending us messages. Thank you, Lord, for letting me be here today to gain a little more health, a little more wisdom and a little more love.' If you could only tune in your receivers to some of those waves you would hear all the heavenly entities speaking to you, telling you about your future, about the wealth you possess, about the life that will be yours when your consciousness is fully awakened. Heaven speaks to you. Heaven

sings to you! After that how can you possibly
say there was nothing there?

The very first being we should turn to in the
morning is the sun, and in that way he will have
a beneficial effect on our whole day. No one
thinks that things of this kind are important any
more. And it's a great mistake. The question of
whom you first meet when you leave home in
the morning is important because some people
bring happiness and success to your day and
others, unhappiness and failure.

When I was still living in Bulgaria – of
course, that was before the last war – there was a
very pretty and touching custom: on New
Year's morning the children were sent out into
the streets and homes in their neighbourhood,
because children are pure and the people be-
lieved that they could bring only good things to
them. Each child had a little branch, sometimes
with ribbons on it, and he was supposed to touch
people with his branch and wish them good
health, success, a good harvest, and so on. The
people thanked them and gave them fruit or
sweets and buns which the children put into the
bags they had with them, and their bags were often bigger than the children!

And when I was a child I used to do that too.
Carrying my little branch, I went and wished a
happy New Year to all the neighbours. I don't

know why, but they thought I could bring blessings on them, and many families asked my
Mother to send me very early in the morning,
before the other children. So she used to wake
me up and dress me and, of course, I didn't enjoy that part of it at all because I was sleepy and
I had to go out in the cold and snow. You know,
the winters in the mountains of Macedonia are
not what they are in the South of France! But I
did it anyway. And, half asleep, I went into each
house to touch the people with my little branch
while I mumbled some words that I had learned
by heart without even understanding what they
meant! But still, it was a nice custom!

It is the same for the sun. He must be the
first, in the morning, to come in to greet you and
wish you good morning... and all your affairs
will prosper! That is why it is so important for
you to get ready the day before, remembering
that next morning you are going to find yourself
in the presence of the finest and most perfect servant of God, that you are going to drink to your
fill of his light, his warmth and his life. Try to
leave all your worries and torments to one side
so as to put yourself totally at the disposal of the
divine world and enter into communion with the
beneficial forces within and all around you.

Now that man has found the way to make
contact by radio, look at how many people can

communicate with each other! If someone is in danger on the sea or in the air, on a mountain or in a cave, he can call for help. Every day we receive messages by radio from all over the world. That's excellent! But why communicate exclusively with human beings? All we hear from them is the clamour of their demands, their revolt, their threats. We should use the receivers God has given us to communicate with the sun and all those beings who are more advanced than we are, to get on to their wavelength and enter into their aura, into their happiness, light and peace. And once we are stronger, thanks to our contact with them, then we need not fear to establish contact with other poor wretches like ourselves.

Some of you are wondering, 'When is he going to stop? He keeps talking about the sun and, in the meantime, it's burning us.' All the better! Then you'll be cooked and ready to eat! For, you know, there are intelligent spirits who are like gardeners: they come and visit your garden or orchard to pick the fruit and have a feast. They exclaim with delight, 'Oh, that lovely melon, that peach! What delicious fruit!' Yes. When they see a human being who is at last waking up to the spiritual life they take care of him and rejoice in all the light that emanates

and radiates from him. All men and women are
visited by heavenly 'gardeners' in this way.
Some may say, 'But I have nothing to give. I'm
not an orchard. How can anyone come and harvest something from me?' In point of fact there
is always some element that can be used in
everyone... even poisonous plants give their poi-
son for medicines!

But if I let myself go and start talking about
this I'll never stop. It is the most fascinating topic. Human beings simply cannot imagine that
they are visited by the inhabitants of the other
world. Even very young girls and boys are visited. Everyone! Because they are like laboratories, filled with chemical elements. But it is not
yet the moment to talk about this at any length.
I'm waiting for you to have done some prepara-
tory work, at least on the most elementary and
fundamental aspects, otherwise you will be unable to assimilate the more important, difficult
aspects. When I see that you are still not capable
of remaining awake while the sun is rising I'm
not going to lead you into areas which demand
the greatest possible mastery of all one's
thoughts and energies.

In the spiritual life, even more than in other
areas, it is dangerous to try to go too fast. If I
gave you a talisman which would enable you to
call up spirits at will, you are still so weak and

inexperienced that you would be destroyed. And what good would I have done you? You will not be ready until you take all these subjects very seriously. For the moment you judge them to be insignificant and unimportant. All right, so they're not interesting! But they can save your lives, whereas the things you do find interesting will bring you nothing but misfortune if they are given to you too soon.

Every year, in the Spring, the sun begins to warm the ground and seeds snuggled deep in the soil awake from their silent sleep when they feel the sun caressing and calling to them, inviting them to arouse themselves and begin their work. You may well scoff and say that germination and growth are an automatic, unconscious mechanism in plants and, of course, I am fully aware of that. But, nevertheless, there is a form of life dormant in plants in the Winter which stirs in the Spring and begins to move in response to the call of the sun. Seeds start pushing up out of the soil and men rejoice because they see that they are going to have a good harvest and enough to eat.

You are thinking that you have known that since you were at school! I have no doubt, but I still say it because I want to show you that you have never really understood it. You know, you know! Yes, but you have never understood. Knowledge and understanding are two different things. People know... but what has all that knowledge done for them so far? Nothing! If you had understood you would have realized that you, too, have seeds in you that you have to tend and make grow.

In the souls and spirits, the minds, hearts and physical bodies of men, the Creator has planted seeds (gifts, virtues, magic powers, spiritual splendours), that only the light and warmth of the sun can make grow. If we go to see the sun rise – the sun, who is the most perfect image of the Creator – every morning during Spring and Summer, it is to give our seeds the best possible conditions for their growth and flowering. As for those who think themselves too intelligent and knowledgeable to indulge in this practise: the divine seed within them will remain buried for eternity.

So, expose yourselves every morning to the sun's rays and all your seeds will begin to sprout. You will become a garden full of lovely flowers and delicious fruit! Fruit that gets no sunlight stays green, bitter and sour, but when it is exposed to the sun it becomes colourful, sweet and delicious. Everybody knows that and, here again, no one has seen that it is equally true for human beings. Of course, I know that a lot of people expose themselves to the sun on the beaches, but more often than not they do so in the afternoon when the sun's rays are no longer beneficial and can even be harmful.

It is in the morning, very early, that you should expose yourself to the rays of the sun and let them do their work. If you do so you will feel the little shoots and buds beginning to grow. When this happens, of course, you are going to have to water them, because if you don't they will be too dry. The sun provides light and warmth but he cannot water your plants for you. He needs water as a collaborator and that collaborator is in us. The sun does part of the work, but we have to do our part which is to water the plants that the sun has warmed. And what do we use for water? Our love, our faith, our trust and good will. We must give the sun a helping hand! If you let him warm you without taking an active part in his work you will never get very good results because the plants that spring up in response to his work will wither and die from lack of water.

But how can one take an active part in the work of the sun? Well, when you are there, exposed to the rays of the sun, you must be active too, just as he is; that is, you must meditate, contemplate, pray and give thanks to the Lord or, if you prefer, pronounce some positive, luminous words. In this way you water those little sprouts in your heart with your love and they will get off to a good start. Learn to become the gardeners of your own little plot of land.

3

SEEKING THE CENTRE

I

Everything that now exists on earth existed
in the first place in its etheric state, in the sun.
We can understand this better if we realize that
the elements are formed by a series of condensa-
tions. In the beginning there was fire. The fire
emanated a substance denser than itself which
was air and the air emanated the substance of
water. In its turn, water rid itself of its heavier
elements, thus forming earth (we now have
scientific proof that all life on earth originated in
water). Each element, then, is a condensation of
another more subtle element: air is a condensation of fire, water of air and earth of water. But
beyond the fire that we know exists another fire,
the light of the sun, which is the true origin of all
things.

You might ask, 'What happened to make all
these elements condense?' What happened is
that they left the centre, the sun, and once they
had left the sun and gone outward towards the

periphery they began to condense and become opaque and heavy. And that is exactly what happened with man: when he left the centre, God, he became dense and dark and in order to retrieve his purity and light he must return to the centre. Now you see how all the precepts of all religions converge in this seeking of the centre or, symbolically speaking, the sun.

Many years ago there was a fun fair near Saint-Cloud called Luna Park. One day I went there and I shall not tell you about all the different things they had for the amusement of the public, only about one thing that was called the 'butter dish' or rotor. It was a large circular platform, mounted on a central axis. When people got onto it they started up the motor and the platform began to spin, faster and faster. Before long those who had stayed near the outside edge were bowled over by the centrifugal force and swept out towards the edge, whereas those who had stayed close to the centre were able to remain calmly where they were! This is a good illustration of the fact that the further you go from the centre the more you come under the influence of the forces of chaos and disorder until, little by little, you lose your balance and your peace of mind. On the other hand, when you get closer to the centre the movement changes and you feel yourself gaining in security, joy and gladness.

It was by the observation of things like this in nature and within themselves that the Initiates of the past managed to discover a whole science and philosophy and elaborate certain methods. Their research and discoveries have been handed down to us and I am giving them to you now so that you can use them to perfect yourselves. However, you have to learn to understand my language. I have been given something that is really a privilege, and that is the ability to use a very clear, simple language which may even seem childish when compared to the abstract, obscure language of philosophers and theologians. But why not simplify the expression of the great truths? Why should they not be made accessible even to children? This is a gift that God has given me: to be able to present the most abstract things clearly and simply, and that is what I am doing for you, every day. Look at the image of the rotor for example: it shows us that if we contemplate the sun in the morning with the desire to get right into him, as it were, not only shall we draw great strength from him but, at the same time, we shall find our own inner centre. We shall leave the outer edge and return towards the source in peace, light and freedom.

The sun is the centre of the solar system and

all the planets gravitate around him in harmonious movement. We must try to impress this same harmonious movement on our cells but to do so we have to get back to the Centre within us, the Spirit, God Himself. Once we do this, all the separate pieces of our lives fall together in harmony with the rhythm of universal life, and the feelings and states of mind we experience are indescribably wonderful; no words can do them justice.

You may wonder if it is really necessary for you actually to go and see the sun rising. Wouldn't it come to the same thing if you prayed at home? Well, of course, you can establish the contact with the Lord, pray to Him and centre yourself in Him perfectly well in your own room. But if, while you pray you can also breathe in pure air and expose yourself to the rays of the sun, then you can unite yourself to God not only intellectually and spiritually through the power of thought but also physically, thanks to the air and light. Here, at sunrise, we have the help of some very powerful factors: the pure air, the freshness and tranquility of the morning, all that space and warmth around us and the rays of the sun. Don't we have all we could possibly desire? If you learn to use all these favourable conditions and make the most of them, your progress towards that central source of life will be much more rapid and effective and much more wonderful.

All creatures without exception have this need to return to centre. They understand it in different ways, of course, but in fact everyone is looking for God. Those who over-indulge in food and drink, those who are forever running after women without ever being satisfied, those who want wealth, power, knowledge : they are all looking for God. My interpretation may well shock religious people, who are often bigoted and narrow-minded, and they may say, 'It's not possible for people to seek God in such devious ways'. But it is perfectly possible! There is no creature in existence who is not looking for God, but each one understands this in his own way.

If we knew where God was and the most perfect way to reach him, that would make everything much easier. But God does exist, just a little, in food and drink. He does exist a little in money. He can be found in men and women. Who else but God could give us such a feeling of fulfilment, gladness and wonder? The thirst for power and authority is a thirst for something that is an attribute of God. The desire to be beautiful is also a desire for the divine attributes of glory and splendour. Even gluttons who spend their days stuffing themselves would not find the pleasures of the palate or the stomach so delectable if there were not some trace of God there. Nothing good, beautiful or delectable exists which does not contain some small particle of the Divinity. However, this does not mean that I am recommending that you take these costly and questionable ways to find God. There are people, even, who look for Him in cesspools. No! The best way, the way that leads straight to God, is the sun.

The very first thing you have to do, then, is to realize the importance of the centre and to understand how, when we seek it, important things begin to change in us, even if we don't feel anything. The nearer we get to the sun with our spirit, our soul, our thought, our heart and our will, the nearer we come to the centre which is God. On the physical level the sun is the visible, tangible representative of the Divinity. All those abstract, distant titles that people use when they speak of God: Prime Cause, Almighty God, Universal Soul, Cosmic Intelligence... all of this is contained in the image of the sun, so real and so close. Yes, we can consider the sun as the epitome, the summary and synthesis of all these sublime, abstract notions that are beyond our grasp. On the physical, material level, the sun is the door, the link and the medium thanks to which we can make contact with the Lord.

Begin by understanding that when you turn to the centre of the solar system you are restoring an identical system within yourself, a system in which your own sun, your spirit, returns to its rightful place and takes command. Up to now, everything is in a mess. Chaos reigns within you! There is no head, no government. All your 'lodgers' eat, drink and kick up a din, vandalizing everything: your thoughts, feelings and desires all contradict each other, all try to have everything their own way. How can you possibly solve your problems in the midst of this anarchy? It's simple: you cannot!

You have to begin by being, internally, like the solar system in which everything gravitates around the centre. But the centre within you must be luminous and alive. You must no longer accept a centre that has become dull, feeble, soiled and inactive. Come on, now! Get to work and clean things up! And then, take a good look at all those that you accepted as your guides in the past. Examine them, one after the other, with the question, 'Are you as luminous as the sun? No? All right, out you go! And you, are you as warm as the sun? No? You, too: out!' Once you have cleaned the place up you can bring in the sun and install him in his rightful place. And when the sun comes into you, when he has found his place in the centre, when he is truly present, real and alive within you, then you will see what he is capable of! When the sun arrives all your inhabitants will feel that their leader, their Lord and master has come home.

Look at children in a classroom, singers in a choir or soldiers in barracks: as long as the 'boss' is not there, the teacher, the choirmaster or the captain, everyone does as he pleases. But as soon as the 'boss' comes in, everyone goes back to his place and they all get down to work together. Or look at a family in the midst of a quarrel: unexpectedly a dear and much-respected friend turns up and in no time at all everyone has put on a smiling face and it is, 'Hello! How are you? Do sit down. We're so glad to see you!' And they even try to smile at each other so that their friend will not realize that they were in the middle of a family row. Why not use the same law and install in yourself the most luminous, the warmest and most vitalizing of all possible 'captains': the sun? Once we do that, instinctively, as though by magic, each part of us will go back into place because it would be ashamed to behave badly in front of such a friend and superior.

When quarrels, tumult and revolution break out within you, if you begin to pray very ardently, everything calms down at once and peace and joy are restored. This is because a friend has come into your house and, thanks to him, all your inhabitants calm down. Have you not all had that experience many times? And now, if you pray to that friend even more fervently and persistently, asking him never to leave you again, to stay and dwell in you forever, to be enthroned in your very centre once and for all, then peace and light will reign eternally within you.

II

If you put your trust in appearances and look at things from the earth's point of view, you will naturally find that the sun rises, sets and revolves round the earth. This example is sufficient to make us realize that those who are accustomed to seeing things from the point of view of the earth, who, in other words, have a geocentric outlook, cannot help but be in error. The whole of their philosophy is false since it is based on the illusion that the sun revolves round the earth. Initiates, on the other hand, know that it is the earth that revolves round the sun and this gives them a totally different point of view: they take up their position on the sun, they look at all things from this point of view and they see the Truth.

Of course you will say, 'Everybody knows that the earth revolves round the sun.' Yes. You know it in theory, but in practice you behave as though it were the sun that revolved round the earth. And that is why I keep telling you, 'As long as you don't try to find the centre, your own centre which is the divine in you, as long as you don't live in that centre, seeing everything and acting only from that centre, you will never find Truth and you will always see everything in a false light.'

If you cannot understand what I am saying, it is because you do not know that the sun and the earth both exist within every man. The earth represents man's instincts and appetites, and the sun represents his mind, his intelligence. Unfortunately, men have lived on the lower levels of their being for centuries. They see everything from the instinctive level, that is, from the material point of view. Nothing else really matters to them. And this is why there are such tremendous obstacles in the way of anyone who tries to bring human beings back to their true centre : the mind, intelligence, light ; anyone who tries, in other words, to get them to abandon their geocentric point of view and adopt the heliocentric point of view. How can one make people understand that by reaching the centre of the solar system, they are at the same time reaching their own centre, their own true core around which everything else should revolve. As long as man persists in wanting to be the hub and centre of his own existence he will, in fact, continue to revolve round something exterior to himself, and be forever tossed hither and thither, forever tormented, and incapable of finding Truth.

I shall use all the means, all the arguments, all the knowledge at my command to bring you to a realization of this overwhelming truth : that you *must* work to reach, first of all, the centre of the planetary system from which all life flows : the Sun, and then, on the spiritual level the supreme, all-powerful Centre : God Himself. And this you must do in order to make a link with your own centre, your own little spark, your higher Self, with the one Centre ; this is the only way for you to find yourself, to discover Truth. You are still living in illusion and torment because you have not yet found your true centre, you have not yet learned to revolve round it, to melt into it. You are still revolving round your desires and whims, your lower appetites. It is not they that should rule your lives! From now on, they must revolve round you, submit to you and be at your service. If it is you who try to satisfy their demands, not only will you be faced with an impossible task, but you will end by losing everything you have. It is they that must be at your service and work for you, for it is you who are their centre, their leader, the head of your own kingdom.

So, what matters most of all is to change your point of view. Instead of grumbling that there is nothing to be gained from getting out of bed to see the sunrise, or that your brain is too muzzy to meditate, now that you know what a wealth of treasure is waiting to be explored, you can get up in the morning in a totally different frame of mind.

Just to make all this a little clearer, let me interpret for you a page out of the Living Book of Nature: if you observe human beings, you see that instinctively, they feel the compulsion to climb the rungs of the social ladder to reach positions of authority and responsibility. In order to satisfy their ambitions they are obliged, periodically, to pass exams and it is only when they have given proof of their worth that they may be chosen for the highest positions. How is it that people have never seen that it is exactly the same system in the spiritual domain ? Initiates and true disciples know very well that other examiners, other juries are there to observe how they solve the problems that life offers, and so they work very hard inwardly, and if they pass their exams they are promoted and given more extensive powers. The higher they climb and the closer they get to the summit, to perfection, the more diplomas they receive from Heaven and the more they are entrusted with important tasks until, one day, they are given all powers. When they reach this level they can command even the forces of Nature, but always and only for good.

And so, instead of vying with others for high positions, instead of competing for the post of magistrate, minister or president, work at raising your inner self so as to reach the sun. The more you love and understand the sun, the more you will raise yourself to the higher levels of your being and the nearer you will come to the summit. Looked at from another angle the summit is identical with the centre, for the geometrical projection of a cone is a circle with a point in the centre. So you see, whether we speak of moving towards the centre of your own circle, your soul or your spirit, or of climbing upwards towards the summit, towards the sun, it is really the same thing. And the benefits that you will receive are also the same: peace, illumination, power and love.

4

THE SUN, OUR PROVIDER

I

The sun is the father of all the planets. They all came from him. That is why everything that exists on earth in the way of chemical elements or minerals and vegetable substances already exists in a more subtle, etheric, form in the sun. The question is to find out how, by concentrating on the sun, we can capture, in their original purity, all the elements we need for our mental and physical well-being. For as long as we continue to look for remedies only on the lower, physical plane and make no effort to rise above this plane, we shall gain nothing on the spiritual level.

At the slightest sign of illness, most people swallow quantities of medicine. It is perfectly true, of course, that the elements that go to make up these medicines come from the sun in the first place. But if people would only make the effort to absorb them on the etheric level, at their source, they would get much more benefit from them. Modern medicine knows nothing yet about these subtle elements, precisely because they are too subtle. But they are far more important than all those that have been discovered to date.

At the moment, orthodox medicine attributes the essential role in health to the endocrine glands, but the truth is that there are other factors, in the astral and mental planes, which trigger and govern the functioning of the endocrine glands. When something goes wrong in the body because the endocrine glands are producing too many or too few hormones, there must be a cause, and where should we look for that cause if not on the astral and mental levels? These two regions, where thoughts and feelings are born, have not yet been explored nor mastered and yet, when part of our system is disturbed, whether it be the endocrine glands or the central or sympathetic nervous system, the ganglions or anything else, we should look for the root cause of this disturbance on the astral and mental planes. In other words, the causes as well as the remedies of disease should be sought on a much higher level than at present. Little by little, science will discover these causes.

Not so long ago we were told, 'If you take such and such quantities of proteins, fats and carbohydrates, such and such mineral salts, every day, that will give you so many calories which will supply you with so much energy.' And calories were thought to be all-important until someone discovered that there were other, more subtle, more imponderable things to be considered: vitamins. From then on, vitamins were all the rage, and everybody stuffed themselves with vitamins. But Initiates do not need to take vitamins. Through their spiritual activity they can absorb other, much more subtle and far more efficient elements which regulate the whole physical system, including the assimilation of vitamins. And now, more recently, hormones have been discovered. But they are not the last word either.

The last word, as I have already said, is our thoughts and feelings. Our thoughts and feelings are forces which set in motion certain functions which, in turn, act on the whole body (the endocrine glands, the nervous system, etc.) and produce harmonious or chaotic results depending on the nature of the original thought or feeling. A few researchers are seeking along these lines already, but no one listens to them. In the future, however, doctors will adopt their theories; research will explore exclusively these subtle factors of men's thoughts and feelings; new branches of study will be created, with laboratories and special techniques, and everyone will be obliged to recognize that esoteric science has always had a solid foundation in truth.

And now, let me tell you how you can receive the etheric particles that the sun sends us in the morning. It is very simple. It is not even worth knowing which elements you need to improve your health: it doesn't make any difference. All you have to do is to raise yourself, mentally, to the most subtle regions and there, you expose yourself and you wait. It is then that your soul and spirit, which are very competent chemists and doctors, and which know the exact nature and properties of all the etheric substances, absorb whatever you need and leave the rest aside. You must just wait – in an attitude of love, submission, joy and trust – and before long, when you come back from the sunrise, you will feel that something within you has been soothed and strengthened and restored to health.

It does not matter if, for the time being, you do not know what these elements are, exactly. But one thing I can tell you in a few words, and that is that they are all present in prana. Prana is a living force. It is the vitality that comes from the sun and that we breathe in with the air and absorb through all our cells. Prana is comparable to water flowing from the heights of a mountain, to a great river flowing from the sun to us, in which, through breathing and meditation, we are able to find all the elements we need.

Those who prefer just to open their mouths and swallow a pill should be warned that this is no more than a harmful, detrimental solution to their problems, because it prevents them from developing their will-power and can only bring them temporary, superficial relief. It will not give a lasting or deep-seated improvement. I do not say that you should never take medicines. But never do so without having first of all absorbed their vital, spiritual elements from prana, for the spiritual and psychic effort that this demands of you strengthens your will and establishes a contact between you and the higher regions. It also stimulates and sets in motion certain centres which prepare the ground, so that, when you do take the physical medicine it has a much stronger and more lasting effect.

So, what I recommend is a combination of both: the chemist's remedy and the spiritual remedy. But I give priority to the spiritual remedy. Obviously, as I have said, medicines contain vegetable and mineral substances which come from the sun in the first place and if God has placed these elements in nature it is in order that we should use them. Of that there is no doubt. But to believe that this is the only way, and that only chemical remedies will put you back on your feet, is contrary to esoteric science.

You may say, 'That's all very well, but those particles we pick up at sunrise are too tiny to be measured. They can't be very effective.' It is true that they are imponderable but they contain the vital quintessence that the sun diffuses throughout the Universe. And the fact that homœopathic medicine knows that very diluted doses are often far more effective than highly condensed ones, goes to prove the truth of what I say. Why not absorb the imponderable, diluted particles, those very subtle 'vitamins' that the sun sends us?

There are all kinds of energies in the sun other than those which can be harnessed to make electricity or heat, and we can draw on them. The sun's energy, if we know how to draw on it, can give us not only vitality and health, but also peace, intelligence and love. But with this philosophy we are far ahead of the rest of humanity. Some people have noticed this. They say, 'With your ideas, you're several centuries ahead of everybody else.' It is true. And what we believe today will be accepted by the whole world in the future.

II

Human beings have a physical body in which the cells are completely renewed every seven years. Knowing this we might ask, 'Since the cells are constantly being renewed, how is it that we still have the same bad habits, the same weaknesses and diseases?' The reason is that the new cells are influenced by the imprints already engraved into the living matter of our being, and they are obliged to follow the old, established ways. That is why our new cells are unable to change our temperament or to rid us of our weaknesses.

Compare this phenomenon with the way any business or factory functions. From time to time, because of illness, old age or death, members of the personnel have to leave and new people who are younger and stronger are employed to replace them. The new employees do the same work as their predecessors, the people change but the jobs remain the same. This is exactly

what happens with the new cells that are produced in us, thanks to nutrition, respiration,
thoughts and feelings and so on. And that is
why, if we want the new cells to be really new
and to produce new results, we have to orient
them differently and give them other imprints. I
have given you many exercises designed to do
just that.

In point of fact, the most effective method for
renewing the materials we are made of is to work
with the sun, and I will explain how. Every
morning, you are there, enjoying the light of the
sun as it pours out into space luminous particles
of extraordinary purity. What is to prevent you
from concentrating all your energies on discard-
ing the particles of your physical and psychic being which are diseased, lack-lustre and worn out,
and substituting new particles direct from the
sun? This is one of the most useful exercises you
can do at sunrise: by means of your thoughts
and your imagination, try to draw some of these
divine particles into yourself. In this way, little
by little, you will completely renew all the materials of your being. Thanks to the sun you will
think and act as a child of God.

Illness is nothing but an accumulation of foreign matter in the body, and if you want to cure
your body you have to clean out that foreign

matter. This is what health really is: purity. And the reason why it is so important for us to harvest the sun's particles every morning is because they are the only ones that leave no impurities or waste of any kind. Everything you eat, drink and breathe necessarily leaves some waste. Only the sun's rays are of such a nature as to leave no waste. That is why we have to learn to nourish ourselves with that higher element: light.

If I ask you how long a human being can survive without eating, you will say, 'Forty , fifty, sixty days or more.' And how long can you go without drinking? 'Ten or fifteen days.' And how long can you live without air? 'Only a few minutes.' From this it is clear that solid food (which corresponds to the element earth) is less important for man than liquid food (which corresponds to the element water), and that liquid is even less important than the gaseous element: air. And now, if I ask how long a man can survive without fire, you will say, 'Oh, years! There are people who have lived for years with no heating.' But I'm not talking about that kind of fire. I'm talking about the inner fire. At the very instant a man loses that inner fire, he dies. As soon as a man's heart loses its warmth, he ceases to live. Fire, therefore, is the element that is most important to man and that is why he

must learn to nourish it and keep it alive within
him.

This is something new! Human beings are
accustomed to nourishing themselves only with
solid, liquid and gaseous elements. And what do
they do with the fourth element: fire and light?
Nothing, or next to nothing! They have not
learned how to nourish themselves with light...
and yet it is even more necessary to them than
air. So, all those who criticise and ridicule us because we go to watch the sunrise every morning
are simply showing their ignorance and stupidi-
ty. We go to the sunrise in order to nourish ourselves with light. Instead of laughing at us they
would do far better to do the same! Man needs
to feed on light in order to nourish his brain.
The brain, too, needs food! And its food is light.
Light awakens those faculties that give man access to the spiritual world. As long as he continues to nourish his brain only with solid, liquid or
gaseous elements (which the brain needs least),
man's understanding will be very limited, he
may understand material things but he will
never be able to grasp the mysteries of the Universe.

You may say, 'Yes, but when we eat and
drink we're feeding the brain as well as all the
rest.' This is true, but you are feeding only the
least subtle part of the brain. For the brain is

composed of several different zones divided according to a hierarchy of functions. Some contain centres which enable man to make his way amongst the realities of the physical and intellectual worlds but others have centres capable of penetrating the realities of the spiritual world. If you learn to nourish your brain with the subtle element, light, the results will be different. Tradition tells us that one day Zoroastra asked the god Ahura Mazda how the first man was nourished, and Ahura Mazda replied, 'He ate fire and drank light.'

Perhaps you will say, 'That's all very fine, but it may take centuries to replace all our old particles.' Not necessarily! You can accelerate that transformation by the intensity of your love. The more you love light, the more you will attract it to you. The majority of human beings are as totally unconscious of the sun as they are of their food. They never worry about *how* they eat. Even if they spend meal-times talking, gesticulating or arguing, they think that their body will absorb and sort out the elements it needs to function correctly. And, of course, it is true that the body does this. But what they do not know is that their food contains subtle elements and forces, drawn from space, and that it is only if they eat consciously that they can be absorbed. These elements, which belong to the etheric, as-

tral and, even to the mental planes, can help us
to improve our thoughts and feelings and our be-
haviour. This is a fact. But on condition that we
eat intelligently and in all consciousness.

And it is exactly the same thing when you go
to the sunrise. If you sit there and think of all
kinds of other things, you will receive some
slight benefit on the physical level from the sun's
light and warmth, but you will not receive the
subtler elements that could help you in your
spiritual evolution. If you are conscious that
through his rays the sun is sending you his own
love, wisdom and beauty, his own life, then you
are preparing yourself to receive these gifts. You
are opening up thousands of little doors through
which the sun's rays can come in and bring you
their treasures. And, in this way you fill your
whole being with the benefits of the sun.

So now you can see why it is so important to
be conscious of what the sun represents. It is
only on this condition that you will be in a position to receive the elements that will help you to
penetrate the laws and mysteries of nature and
to experience peace and happiness.

5

THE SOLAR PLEXUS

The light, warmth and life that we know, here on earth, are a very inferior reflection of true light, true warmth and true life. Behind the light of the sun is the Light of God. But we can have no knowledge of this Light, any more than we can know His Warmth, His Love or His Life, that is, the most intense degree of life. God is utterly unknowable, incomprehensible for man and yet, at the same time, He almost touches us, although in a very remote and less perfect form. You must not think of the light of the sun as the true Light of God. It is a reflection of the true Light. That other Light, that we can neither know nor comprehend is so subtle, so tremendously potent that, for us, and even for many creatures of the spirit world who are far more advanced than we, it is darkness.

In Initiatic Science it is said that 'out of darkness came forth light.' In the beginning was chaos, unorganized matter or *hyle* as it is called in Greek. This original chaos is represented by a circle: zero. Symbolically, the circle represents infinite, inanimate matter. But it is very difficult for us to understand these notions, particularly if we try to do so on the purely intellectual level: the human intellect is virtually incapable of grasping these truths. And this explains why philosophers and scholars who try to understand everything with their intellects fail really to understand. When it is a question of theories, all right! The brain can cope. But really to understand things, that is, to feel, taste and live them, is not within the scope of the brain.

You have often heard the saying that it is the heart that understands. Even the Gospels refer to the heart as the seat of understanding. But what heart are they referring to? People think it means the physical heart, the organ that pumps blood. No. The true heart, the heart according to the Initiates, is the solar plexus. It is the solar plexus that feels, understands and grasps the great cosmic truths. The brain is capable only of arguing, writing, talking and bragging about its knowledge, without having any clear idea of reality. Look at the way it is in the world today, the world of the fifth race: people explain, talk and write books but, in reality, they have not understood what they are talking about for the simple reason that their brains are incapable of perfect understanding. One has to live things to understand them, to *live* them with one's whole being.

The solar plexus governs all the functions of the physical body: respiration, elimination, circulation, nutrition and growth. And it is also by means of the solar plexus that man can enter into a true communication with the Universe, because the solar plexus is linked to the entire Universe, and this is not the case for the brain. In actual fact, communication between the brain and the Universe could be established, but the brain is not yet sufficiently developed, for it is of very recent formation. The solar plexus, on the other hand, was formed much longer ago and it in turn formed and nourished the brain. The brain is the offspring of the solar plexus, and that is why it sends the brain sustenance and support; when it ceases to do so, a person becomes tired and sleepy, his head aches and he is unable to think clearly.

The brain is not cut off from the solar plexus; if it cannot always fully benefit from the support offered by the solar plexus, it is because it has not yet learned to communicate correctly with it. I have already explained to you that the solar plexus is a brain in reverse. In the brain, the grey matter is on the outside and the white matter on the inside whereas in the solar plexus, the grey matter is on the inside and the white matter on the outside. Also, I have already explained that it is the grey matter that enables us to think and the white matter that enables us to feel. Thanks to the white matter which is on the outside, the solar plexus feels all that goes on in a man and in each of his cells. And that is why it works ceaselessly to restore order, whereas the brain doesn't even notice that anything is wrong until it has become very serious and everything grinds to a halt. And even then, it is incapable of remedying the situation. For example, if your heart beats too fast or too slowly, or if you have a stomach ache, the brain is powerless to help. Besides, it is not its job! Whereas if the solar plexus has the proper conditions it needs in order to function normally, it can set everything right. It has an extraordinary pharmacy at its disposal that you cannot begin to imagine. And as it is in contact with all the organs of the body and all your cells, it knows what is going on and can intervene. So it is far better equipped than the brain. But all of this has never been properly explained, even by medical science.

The brain came into existence very late, both in animals and in human beings. In fact, the ant's brain is far better organized than man's because ants have existed for longer than men. When one compares the brain of an ant with that of man, one is astounded to see how ants have managed to organize such a tiny brain. The human brain is not yet fully organized, but it will be eventually, because its mission is to take in the total sum of all knowledge; it is designed to achieve fantastic results. But, I repeat: the organ which guides and governs at the moment and on which all others depend, is the solar plexus, together with the Hara centre situated a little lower down, for the two are associated.

Westerners are destroying themselves because they centre all their activity in the brain: study, calculations, stress, etc. As the brain is not equipped to stand up to such great tension, much of the nervous illness of our time comes from its being overworked. If Westerners knew how to share out the work between the brain and the solar plexus they would never be tired, because the solar plexus never tires: it is an almost inexhaustible reservoir. But if someone lives a disordered life the solar plexus is prevented from functioning correctly. It feels constricted, jammed, the nerves are ill. Someone who lives a disordered life is in the process of destroying this most precious element, the one on which his whole system depends.

In the ancient treatises on alchemy there is constant reference to a kind of oil or essence that possessed marvellous properties: it could give health, intelligence, beauty, knowledge and so on. In point of fact, all living things, plants, animals and men, can distill this essence. It has been variously called the true sap, prana, the Elixir of eternal life, etc. Some people call it magnetism. This is what Jesus was referring to when he said, 'From his belly will flow streams of living water.' And when men eat and breathe (for the air is full of the essence distilled by the sun and we can receive it when we breathe), and when they think, they are trying to distill this oil or essence.

As I have already told you, this essence can be found everywhere. Plants draw it from the soil, the air and the sun's rays and, thanks to it they produce their sap. The sap of plants is a symbol of the living sap that flows in us. And where is the spring from which it flows? In the solar plexus. Sometimes, when you are worried or discontented and impatient, if you are sufficiently sensitive to what goes on within you, you can feel that your solar plexus is drained. The solar plexus contains living magnetism and when it is upset and the magnetism escapes, you feel that your strength has left you and that you are incapable either of action or of concentration.

On the other hand, if you are happy and

calm you can feel your solar plexus at ease, you can feel that something is flowing in it, like a spring. The solar plexus is the reservoir of our vital forces, the accumulator of all our energies, and if you know how to refill it every day you will have a source at hand from which to draw the energies you need at any moment.

And now, here is an exercise to do at sunrise: while you meditate on the light and warmth of the sun, put your right hand on your solar plexus. In this way you fill it with the forces and energies that will enable you to go on with your work without tiring.

6

MAN IS MADE
IN THE IMAGE OF THE SUN

I

When we look at the sun, the first thing we see is a luminous disk which never changes shape or size and which can be observed, measured, photographed and so on. What we see is the sun's body. But if we want to study what emerges from him, the light that pours out from the centre towards the periphery, if we want to know what that light is and how far it reaches out into space, we find ourselves faced with an impossible task. It is quite beyond our imagination.

A human being is built on the same pattern as the sun: he has a clearly defined physical body which does not change. But what do we know about what flows out of him: his thoughts and feelings, his radiations and emanations? Not very much. People have a tendency to take the body for the whole man, but before long they are going to have to revise these pre-conceived notions. They will recognize that only esoteric

science is completely truthful, because it has always taken into account both aspects at once:
the objective, measurable aspect of the material
phenomena which must not be neglected, but
also and above all, the spiritual, living aspect,
the emanations and radiations, the nature and
power of which are still unknown.

I told you one day, that the planets and the
sun touched us, and that surprised you, but it is
true. The sun touches us from afar by means of
his rays. And we, who are built on the same pattern as the sun, have powers that reach far
beyond the bounds of our physical bodies by
means of our thoughts, our soul and our spirit.
Just as the sun acts on metals, plants, animals
and human beings, just as he penetrates, warms
and nourishes them, in the same way, by means
of our emanations, we can transform, improve,
enlighten and vivify creatures who are far from
us.

But let's go further: the luminous disk in the
sky, which is perfectly circumscribed, is the
sun's body. The rays flowing from him are his
thoughts, his soul and his spirit which he sends
out to the periphery to distribute the abundance
of his riches. And when they have discharged
their load of treasure they go back to the sun to
be recharged before going out again, to visit
other creatures in space.

In our bodies, the heart represents the sun : it has the same function, the same untiring activity. Without interruption, the heart continues its work even when the other organs of the body relax a little, because it has only one aim : to help, support, feed, build and repair. It seeks only to give, to be impersonal, generous and full of love. But have human beings ever realized that they possess a vital organ in their own physical bodies, the heart, and that it represents the sun within?

In the same way, the rays of light that the sun sends out correspond to the blood. Like it, they are filled with all that is useful, beneficial, profitable and salutary for all creatures. When the blood has distributed its load of nutritious, invigorating, healing materials to the cells and absorbed their impurities, it returns, but not directly to the sun, the heart : first it goes to the lungs of the universe to be cleansed of those impurities. The planet which corresponds to the lungs is Jupiter. Astrology attributes the role of the liver to Jupiter, the liver has the same function as the lungs in another area : it cleanses and purifies the system of its poisons. In Bulgarian, the liver is called *cheren drob*, which means black lung, whereas the lungs are called *bel drob*, which means white lung. You can see the striking comparison: in two different areas, the task of both organs is to purify.

Although astrology generally links Jupiter with the liver, I attribute this role to Saturn. Mythology can help us to understand the relationship: in the beginning Jupiter was in the liver and Saturn in the lungs, but when Jupiter deposed his father, he took over the government of the lungs and relegated Saturn to the liver. Ever since, Saturn has led an underground life, in the mines, like the liver which works below the diaphragm in darkness, amongst poisons.

But we had better leave all that alone and get back to the sun! So, the light that flows from the sun is his blood. Once the sun's rays have been used by the planets and the innumerable other creatures of the universe (for space is peopled with billions of creatures who receive the light of the sun and find their nourishment in it), they lose some of their light and warmth, and they turn to Jupiter who purifies them (Saturn and the moon both play a part in this process of purification) and finally they return to the sun. Then, once again loaded with love, wisdom, truth and force, the sun's rays are sent out, once again, into the whole universe.

So, you see, the solar system is a living organism with its own circulatory system. The life of the solar system flows from the sun, its heart, which beats tirelessly in order to keep the whole body supplied with the nourishment it needs. And this is why the heart is the symbol of impersonality, disinterestedness and love, because in man, it takes the place of the sun. What makes the sun so luminous and warm is his desire to give, always to give. If you deprive someone of his love and kindness, of his desire to help his fellow men, his face becomes sombre and lacklustre. Look at a man who is on his way to visit a sick or unhappy friend, taking him presents and consolation: his face is radiant and full of beauty. And then look at a criminal who is plotting some nefarious deed: he is sombre, tense and ill at ease: the light has gone out of him. You must learn to understand this language. The stronger your desire to enlighten, instruct and help others, the more the light within you will increase and spread until it forms an extraordinary, brilliant, luminous aura all around you. It is the sun who possesses the true criteria and measures, the absolute laws. And that is why I never try to learn from books: for me, the sun is the only true book.

And now, have you never been surprised that the sun should give and give and radiate as he does, for billions of years, and never be exhaust-

ed? What you do not know is that there is a law
of Divine Love according to which the more you
give, the more you receive. A vacuum cannot
exist in nature. An empty space is immediately
filled by something else. And this law is effective
on all levels. If what you give is luminous, radiant, beneficial, in return you will receive elements of the same quality, with the same luminous, radiant quintessence. But if you emanate
filth, in no time at all your supply of filth will be
replenished.

The sun is inexhaustible because in his desire
to give he constantly receives. He sends out his
rays to us but, at the same time he receives new
energies, ceaselessly, from the Infinite, the Immense, the Absolute. He never ceases to give,
sending out his rays towards the periphery
whilst, in his own central core, he is constantly
absorbing energy from the Absolute. He explained this to me one day, 'I am permanently
tuned in to the Infinite, to the Divinity, and as
my thoughts and desires are perfectly pure, I attract the purest and most luminous energies.
Learn from me how to become perfect, inexhaustible, tireless. Adopt the same aims as I
have. Make it your ideal to be like me and to
work in the same way and you will see that this
is true: if you spend your energies for the good
of others, you will immediately find yourself

filled with new energy.' How does this happen? It is mysterious... but it is true! Whereas if you spend your energies pursuing too personal a goal you will take a long time to recuperate and be strong again. If by some misfortune you fall ill, it will perhaps be months or even years before you are well again. People who are inspired by the purest thoughts and the highest ideal always recover very quickly.

Of course, you will say that it is difficult to attain to the tremendously exalted stature of the sun. That is true, I know. But if human beings perfect and purify themselves and become more spiritual little by little, generation after generation, they will acquire the same qualities as the sun : they will be tireless, invulnerable and radiant.

II

Esoteric science teaches us that no evil spirit has the right to enter the dwelling place of an Initiate. An Initiate can post a notice at his door forbidding evil spirits to enter under pain of such and such a punishment for failing to respect the order. When he wants to perform a magic ritual or an important work, he begins by designating and consecrating a special place in order to prevent evil spirits from entering it; he draws a circle round it, inscribes some sacred names, and then he is free to work in peace. Only superior beings have the right to enter this circle. Lower entities must remain outside no matter how they scream and threaten, and if they attempt to enter they are instantly struck down.

When a human being wants to create, he is like a pregnant woman or a mother bird who is ready to lay her eggs: he needs a nest, a peaceful retreat. In the invisible world it is exactly the same, every spirit has his own place specially reserved for him in infinite space. Every spiritual being dwells in a clearly defined place, protected by certain vibrations or colours or by a particular quintessence. No other being has the right to enter and perturb things with its antagonistic vibrations. Only the highest beings have the right to go wherever they like because theirs is never a disturbing influence.

In the dwellings of humans, millions, even billions of beings come and go at will, moving about without anyone noticing them. If you fail to put up a 'No entry' sign on your door, by which I mean if you fail to consecrate your home, lower entities will see that the door is wide open and will come in and steal. When this happens it is no good complaining to Divine Justice, you will simply be told, 'It's your own fault! You should have put up a fence or at least a notice.'

As your heart, soul and spirit remain wide open to all comers and are not consecrated and protected until you have put up a fence of light, any spirit has the right to come in and dirty everything, vandalize your home and steal your possessions. They cannot be punished for it. It is up to the owner to take steps to prevent this. Just as, in the past, cities and castles were protected by moats, ramparts and draw-bridges, in the same way the disciple must surround himself with walls, ramparts and fortifications. For a disciple, as for an Initiate, the very best form of protection against bad vibrations and the spirits of darkness, is his aura. The more vast and luminous his aura and the greater the purity of its colours, the safer he will be, for the aura acts as a shell, an armour, to protect against all malevolent currents. Do you ever think about developing your aura? No, you leave yourselves wide open to the comings and goings of all kinds of undesirable beings, and then you complain that you have been robbed, that you are worn out, miserable and unhappy.

Look at how everything in nature is on its guard: birds, insects and wild beasts all develop some form of protection against discovery and capture. Why should man be so guileless and trusting as to believe that he will be spared and that no enemy threatens his safety? I assure you, millions of entities are relentlessly at work night and day to bring down humanity. They have sworn to wipe it out completely. Fortunately for humanity it has its protectors, too! It is thanks to them that mankind has not already been wiped off the face of the earth... but it still has to endure much suffering and torment.

The conclusion to be drawn from all this is that you must work to develop your aura. And how can you do this? By going to see the sun rise in the morning. Look at the sun and see how he has wrapped himself in a wonderful aura full of marvellous colours. Say to yourself, 'I, too, want to surround myself with the most beautiful colours.' Close your eyes and imagine yourself clothed in purple light, then in blue, green, yellow, orange and red. Or if you like, begin with the red and work up to the purple, keeping each colour around you for a few minutes. Bathe yourself in this light, imagine that it radiates a long, long way and that all creatures who come within its radius benefit from it, that everybody you meet or who comes into contact with you in one way or another will receive some blessing from it.

This is how your aura can be a protection for you and at the same time a blessing for others. Thanks to your aura you can help others. In fact, this is something you should know: when someone you love is ill, unhappy or discouraged, if you really want to help him, you can send him colours. Oh, yes, there are a great many exercices you can do with your aura and with colours.

7

THE SPIRITS OF THE SEVEN LIGHTS

It is written in the book of Zohar:

'Seven lights are there in the Most-High and therein dwells the Most Ancient of all the Ancients, the Mystery of all Mysteries, the Hidden of all the Hidden Ones: Ain Soph.'

Those seven lights or rays are the seven colours of the spectrum: red, orange, yellow, green, blue, indigo and violet. They are the seven Spirits who stand forever before the throne of God. The colours produced by the prismatic refraction of light therefore also have symbolic significance.

When you look at the sunlight through a prism you discover a world of untold richness and splendour. But how is it that when light, which is one, is passed through a prism, which is three, it becomes seven? One, three and seven! This phenomenon has always intrigued me ever since I was a child, and it has always been a delight to me to see the wealth of beauty and purity contained in the light of the sun. It is this that led me to see that man himself is a prism, a trinity. In order for the light of the sun to be perfectly refracted into the seven colours, it is essential that the three sides of the prism be equilateral as well as perfectly transparent. Similarly, a human being must develop harmoniously the triangle formed by his mind, his heart and his will so that the light of God, the light of the sun, may shine through him and be manifested in all the splendour of the seven colours.

Only disciples and Initiates who have worked to develop their intelligence, who have accustomed their hearts to feel and love correctly and who have become strong through their constant striving, their will to overcome all their negative aspects, only they are able to refract white light into the seven colours, and their aura grows continually in beauty and purity as well as in size.

Those who never properly develop the triangle of their mind, heart and will have only two or three colours in their aura. All the others are absent. And if, by misfortune, they deform their triangle, then their intellect becomes malicious, cunning and aggressive, their heart is filled with hatred, evil, cruelty, they thirst for revenge and sensual pleasures, and their will is at the service of the forces of destruction. When this is the case, their aura not only loses all its vivid, gleaming colours but it becomes full of all kinds of horrors.

Initiatic Science identifies the red ray with the Spirit of Life. The vibrations of red create a bond between human beings and the Spirit of Life. Red has a vivifying effect and enhances vitality. But there are thousands of different shades of red, each one of which represents a different force: love, sensuality, dynamic energy, intoxication, anger, etc.

The orange ray is identified with the Spirit of Sanctity, the second Spirit. By means of orange light, therefore, you can create a bond between yourself and sanctity. But here, too, there are innumerable different shades which may represent dignity, individualism or pride. A certain shade of orange can improve your health, another inspires and strengthens faith, but above all, orange is associated with sanctity and health.

Golden yellow is the Spirit of Wisdom. Its vibrations encourage men to read, reflect and meditate, to seek wisdom and to be guided by reason and prudence in their acts.

The green ray is the Spirit of Eternity and Evolution. Green is the colour of growth and development and also of wealth. It is linked to hope and it helps humans to advance along the evolutionary path.

The blue ray is identified with the Spirit of Truth. It is associated with religion, peace and music. Blue develops the musical sensibilities, pacifies the nervous system, heals the lungs and also has a beneficial influence on the eyes, which are the symbol of truth.

Indigo is identified with the Spirit of Force, the Spirit of Royalty. It has approximately the same properties as blue.

The purple or violet ray is the Spirit of Divine Omnipotence and of Spiritual Love. It is the Spirit of Sacrifice. Purple is a very powerful colour which protects man, a very mystical, very subtle colour which helps the astral body to leave the physical body and travel in other worlds. It also helps him to understand God's love. It is not at all beneficial to plant life.

When I was a boy of fifteen or sixteen, I did a great deal of work with colours. Not only did I picture them in my imagination and meditate on them often, but I used to daub coloured paint on the windows of my room to see what effect they would have on me. I would meditate in the room filled with the coloured light that filtered through the painted glass and, for a few days, I would observe the effects that each colour had on me, then I would wash it off and begin all over again with the next colour. I hardly need to tell you that my parents and the neighbours thought I was going out of my mind! But I continued, unperturbed, to experiment with the different colours. With purple I soared away into other worlds. I even invited some friends in to see what effect that colour had on them and all they did was go to sleep! And all my flowers died. But I still love purple.

When the red in a person's aura is no longer clear and pure, it is because he has given way to anger, drunkenness or sensuality. For each one of these vices the shade of red is different and clairvoyants can readily distinguish them. From time immemorial, red has always been associated with blood and war. It is a beautiful colour but it must be very pure, a shade that when mixed with white, produces a luminous pink.

Pink also expresses love: the white contributes purity and harmony. It has a pacifying influence, when free of violence and egoism, love becomes wiser. It becomes tenderness. That is why pink is seen as the symbol of tenderness, of delicate sentiments. I advise someone who has too much vitality to create a bond with white or to associate with other people who have a lot of white in them, that is to say, who are pure and honest. Then there will at least be a mixture, and the red will become pink. In this way he will no longer be tormented and pursued by the forces of red within him. Pink also has a beneficial effect on the intelligence. We all know that if we say someone wears rose-coloured glasses, it means he is optimistic. Someone who looks at life through rose-coloured spectacles, has a spirit unencumbered by worry or sombre, negative ideas. He sees the good side of life, he is a happy person.

The same general remarks can be made for the other colours: certain shades of blue in a person's aura reveal that he has lost his faith or that he is no longer rooted in peace and truth. If the yellow is dull or discoloured it shows that someone does not follow his reason or that he is incapable of deep thought and understanding; one cannot count on his intellectual capacity. But I do not want to prolong my explanations on this subject, I have other things I want to talk to you about. It is enough if you remember that the Seven Spirits who are forever in the presence of the Everlasting Lord, are the Spirit of Life: Red; the Spirit of Holiness: Orange; the Spirit of Wisdom: Yellow; the Spirit of Eternity: Green; the Spirit of Truth: Blue; the Spirit of Force: Indigo and the Spirit of Sacrifice: Purple.

If you want to produce any particular colour, you can always get it by combining two other colours. For instance, purple and orange will give you red, red and yellow will give you orange, orange and green give yellow, and so on. Each colour is the offspring of two other colours: its father and mother. But if you do not know which colours to mix you will never get good results. And why is this? Simply because the oppositions and affinities that exist between colours, exist also between the planets that correspond to those colours.

Red, for instance, corresponds to Mars. Mars is impetuous, violent and destructive. It represents the masculine principle in all its potency, but only on one plane, for the sun (although, strictly speaking, the sun is not a planet) and Jupiter are also masculine, but on a higher level. Green corresponds to Venus, and people in whom red is the dominant colour, are attracted to those in which green predominates because they set each other off to advantage, and this is wonderful. But if they form a union and fuse with each other they give birth to a monster! They can go for walks together, talk to each other, look at each other and exalt each other's good qualities, but they must not unite, for the mixture of red and green produces a very dirty colour. It is the same with orange and blue: the mixture is horrible, but when you put them side by side, both become more expressive, they bring out the best in each other. Blue corresponds to the planet Jupiter and orange corresponds to the sun and both are positive, or masculine, and that is why they should never marry.

And now, take, for example, yellow and purple which should never be mixed either. Yellow corresponds to Mercury and, according to the Cabbalah, purple corresponds to the moon. However, the moon is usually associated with white, so if we say that the moon is white, then we can attribute purple to Neptune, for Neptune is identical with the moon on a higher plane. Similarly, Uranus is identical with Mercury, but on a higher plane. You will understand these relationships better if you see their position on the Sephirotic Tree of Life.

Mercury (Hod) is in opposition to Uranus (Chokmah). On another axis, Venus (Netzach) is in opposition to Saturn (Binah). On the central pillar, the Moon (Yesod) is in opposition to Neptune (Kether). On the horizontal, Mars (Geburah), which is on the pillar of Judgment is in opposition to Jupiter (Chesed), on the pillar of Mercy. One day I will explain all these relationships to you, and you will see how Venus and Saturn represent almost the same reality manifested in different regions. It is quite possible that this contradicts what you have learned before, but you will see for example, how, on the column of love, the love of Venus becomes the

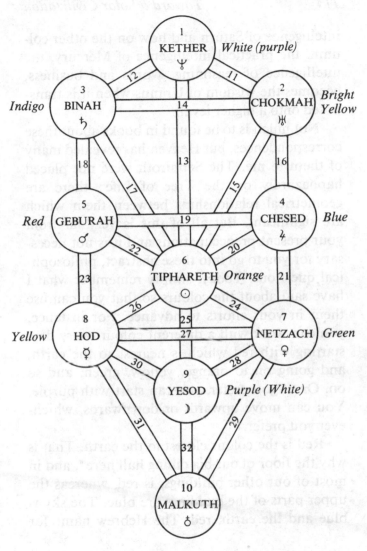

The Sephirotic Tree

intelligence of Saturn and how on the other column, the practical intelligence of Mercury, the intelligence of reasoning, words and business, becomes the wisdom of Uranus when it is transposed onto a higher level.

Not much is to be found in books about these correspondences, but Heaven has revealed many of them to me. The Sephiroth were not placed haphazardly on the Tree of Life: there are geometrical relationships between them which are significant. But all of this is very far from your present preoccupations and it is not necessary for you to go into these abstract, philosophical questions. Today, simply remember what I have said about the colours so that you can use them in your efforts to advance. For instance, you can work with a different colour every day, starting with red which is nearest to the earth, and going on to orange, yellow, green, and so on. Or, if you prefer, you can start with purple. You can move upwards or downwards, whichever you prefer.

Red is the colour closest to the earth. That is why the floor of our big dining hall here*, and in most of our other buildings, is red, whereas the upper parts of the buildings are blue. The sky is blue and the earth, red. The Hebrew name for

* The Bonfin in Fréjus, France.

the first man was *Adam*. The place where he lived was called Eden. The Hebrew word for earth is *Adamah,* and for red: *Adom*. So the words, red, earth, man and Eden, in Hebrew are all formed from the same root. This is why the Cabbalah calls Adam 'the red man.' But the old Adam must die and give way to the new man, the Christ. And Christ is symbolized by blue.

The work of the alchemists was precisely this: to transform red into blue. This simply means that everything that is still rough, violent and brutish in man must be transformed and sublimated. Red and blue are the two opposite poles and if you want to move from one to the other you can consult the alchemists: they will tell you that you have to learn to work with acid and alkali. If you know how to work with the two principles, masculine and feminine, then you will be able to change the colours. You will be able to turn blue into red or red into blue by adding a few drops of acid or of alkali. So, you see, chemistry can throw light on religious precepts, but religious people do not know this. And nor do chemists. For scientists, these are purely physical phenomena and they never attempt to interpret them. Science limits itself to noting facts and never looks for the underlying reason, the deeper significance. I am different: I enjoy interpreting facts for you.

So we are the red Adam who must make way
for the Christ. This transformation is possible : it
is the goal of all religion. The old man, Adam,
subject to his own passions (red), must be replaced by the Christ, the new man (blue), who
dwells in truth, peace and harmony. Blessed are
they who understand! Blessed are they who follow the light!

I will end by quoting those words again from
the Book of Zohar. I love them dearly and often
repeat them to myself:

*'Seven lights are there in the Most High and
therein dwells the Most Ancient of all the Ancients, the Mystery of all Mysteries, the Hidden
of all the Hidden Ones: Ain Soph.'*

Aren't those magnificent words? Repeat
them to yourself often, and 'Let there be light!'
From now on, may all of you work on light, with
light and for light!

8

THE SUN AS OUR MODEL

I

Reading of the Thought for the Day :

'The highest ideal is to take the sun as your model. If you try to imitate a scholar, a philosopher, even a hero, a saint or an Initiate, you will certainly receive some small particles of their virtues and qualities, but never as many or as pure as those you will receive if your model is the sun.

'The image of perfection is the sun and if you adopt him as your model, if, like him, you think of nothing but bringing light, warmth and life to all creatures, then you will really work your own transformation. For even if you never acquire all the light, warmth and life of the sun, the desire to do so is sufficient to project you into heavenly regions where you can really perform wonders. This desire to communicate light, warmth and life to other creatures will make you, yourself, more luminous, more loving and more alive.'

Here, again, we have a text that will scandalize some of you and astonish others. Take the sun as your model? Everyone will say, 'Look, there's no sense to it! The sun isn't a conscious, intelligent being!' And that is just where they are wrong.

Of course, the sun looks like nothing more than a ball of fire. But what about humans, what do they look like? Bodies function like machines, and the whole universe is a machine. There have even been geniuses, from time to time, telling us that the universe is the result of chance. But isn't it a bit strange that chance should be so intelligent and so discerning?

If a machine works it is not the result of chance : there has to be someone who sets it in motion. No one has ever seen a machine start functioning unless an intelligence has set it off.

Wherever there is matter there has to be a spirit to animate it. That is why the notion that the sun is no more than an incandescent ball of fire is an error. The sun is a magnificent land, inhabited by the most highly evolved creatures who rule over the planets. And it is their vibrations which are transformed as they pass through space into light and heat. On the sun itself the temperature is very moderate. The only thing is : who will ever believe me? Children, perhaps?

In saying that we should take the sun as our model I am not belittling any of the great Masters of mankind because they, too, modeled themselves on the sun. The fact that they enlightened the whole world with their wisdom, that they warmed the hearts of all men with their love and that they vivified the whole world with the purity of their lives, all this proves that the sun was their model. Besides, if the sun never ceases to shed light and warmth on us, if he unfailingly sustains life in the universe, it is because he, too, follows the example of a model: the Lord God.

Imitation is an innate tendency in human beings, as it is in all creatures. The problem is whom to imitate? A movie star? A famous football player? People do not have the right criteria to choose their models wisely and, above all, they have not the slightest idea of the importance of this question for their psychic life. Suppose you have a friend: the simple fact that you spend time with him is sufficient for you to pick up some of his particles. He gives you something of his virtues and vices. In this way, without your being in any way aware of it, he is your model. So, in the same way, if you spend time with the sun, marvelling every day at his goodness, his purity, his power, at the abundance of life that flows from him, you will end by noticing that a transformation is taking place within you, in your cells; that something inside you is beginning to vibrate differently, and you become more and more luminous and loving and better able to communicate life to others.

If you want to have a beneficial influence on human beings, tune in to the sun every day so as to receive some of his particles which you can then communicate to others. The sun is the only being who can induce in you the best possible disposition towards mankind.

If we do not keep this model of warmth and light constantly before our eyes, what we manifest will necessarily be very inferior. Just look at how most people behave: everybody tries to profit from others and to use them for their own ends, to subjugate them. It is not a pretty sight! Whereas the sun offers us the image of radiant generosity and this has a good influence on us. Even if he is not endowed with intelligence and reason in the usual sense of these terms, the contact with his light and warmth can only inspire in us more generous thoughts and more brotherly feelings.

Of course, there have always been a few exceptional beings whom we could take for models of purity, goodness, intelligence and integrity. But perfection is something more. Perfection supposes the ideally balanced development of the three factors: mind, heart and will, and it is this that is so rare. There are people who are extraordinarily intelligent and well-informed but they have no love for their fellow men. Others are full of love but they have no will-power, and so on. Life is full of examples of people who are highly developed in one area and lacking in others. Whereas the sun offers the spectacle of the ideal of perfection: his light tells us that he knows everything, his warmth is eloquent proof of his love and the life that flows from him into the whole universe reveals his omnipotence.

When a person wants to learn the trade of a cooper or barber for instance, he goes to someone who knows how to make barrels or trim beards to see how he does it. But when people want to learn how to become immortal, how to attain eternal life, they try to learn from the dead! No one thinks to ask the one being who is really alive! That's human intelligence for you! They think they can learn life from the books of people who are dead and buried. No one goes to the sun. They only use the sun to obtain light and heat and, nowadays especially, to exploit his energy. They want to bottle the sun and sell him! If you try to talk to all those physicists and engineers about taking the sun as their model they will laugh you to scorn. But you, if you listen to me, if you put the sun before all other concerns, you will see for yourselves how he will flood you with light, how he will stimulate and heal you.

But I talk to you about this over and over again and I know very well that some of you will continue to take some little whipper-snapper or some insignificant little damsel as his model! I can hear you ask, 'Do you mean to say we shouldn't have a sweetheart?' Of course you may have a sweetheart, but that is just it: take the sun as your model in your loving. Turn to the sun, fill yourself with his light, and then kiss your sweetheart and you will see how different it is. In reality it would be preferable not to kiss each other, but if you must, then at least, before you do so, fill yourself with the light, warmth and purity of the sun.

As for myself I have never advised you to take me as a model. I have always said that I am simply a signpost. I look towards the sun and point in his direction to show you the way to him. For it is the sun who will give you everything. What can I give you? All I can do is lead you towards the sun, the best example of perfection there is.

Most people think there is nothing better than the work they have chosen: their own particular trade or profession. Well, I believe that nothing can compare to this work, which is still unknown: to become like the sun who illuminates, warms and gives life to all creatures. Yes, take the sun as your example and, like him, spread light, warmth and life around you. Of course, it is not easy to become like the sun. Even several hundred years from now you still will not have managed it. But at least, if you are faithful to your ideal of resembling him, your ideal will produce such a transformation that, inside yourself, you will truly become a reflection of the sun, and in your presence your fellow men will begin to feel more luminous, more loving and more alive.

There are thousands of different occupations in the world, especially in recent years which have seen the creation of so many new professions, but none can be compared to the occupation of someone who has the ambition of becoming like the sun. No other work could ever satisfy him. Look at your own occupations: whatever you do, you are always limited. You may be a chemist, an astronomer, a musician, a painter, a lawyer, an attorney... whatever you may be, part of yourself is fulfilled by your work, but neither your science nor your art will help you solve all the other problems of your life (your wife and children, your friends or even your health).

All those who consciously approach the sun with the desire to resemble him end by bringing life, warmth and sunlight to others. The others, who sense this, are drawn to them. How can you resist someone who makes you feel alive and full of warmth and light when you are with him? Everybody tries to avoid those who are dull, cold and lifeless, and if you can't avoid them, you take care to protect yourself from their influence. Look at the flowers: at night they close their petals, but in the daytime they open up to the sun. Flowers speak to us. They say, 'Hearts can only be opened by warmth and light.' But who understands the language of plants?

Take the sun as your model. Even later in the day when you are no longer in the presence of the rising sun, watch yourself, analyse yourself to see whether you are radiating and spreading light, whether you are warming and delighting the hearts of others, whether you are bringing them life. Every minute of the day, ask yourself this, because it is your key to perfection.

II

The most sublime lesson that the sun gives us is his love for all creatures. He does not worry about who receives his rays. Whether human beings be intelligent or stupid, honest men or criminals, whether they deserve his benefits or not, he pours out his light on all without distinction. In this, the sun is absolutely unique. Take any one of the extraordinary beings who have lived on earth : all of them had some partiality, some preferences, some dislikes. Even the greatest Prophets, even the greatest Masters, never manage to free themselves completely from the need to apply the law of justice and to punish the wicked.

Why does the sun give his light, warmth and love to all creatures without discrimination, as abundantly to criminals as to saints? Is he blind? Can he not see their crimes? Or is he simply a mechanism without intelligence or discernment, who is in no way concerned by the

virtue or the wickedness, by the honesty or the
dishonesty of men? No! The sun sees human
faults and crimes more clearly than anyone else
but, for him, they are just little mistakes, little
deficiencies, little blemishes. He cleanses them,
heals them, washes them, and continues with
unlimited patience to help human beings to
reach perfection.

And so you ask, 'But why such generosity?
What is the sun's philosophy?' Well, I will tell
you. The sun has a certain view of the human
race. He can see the immortality and the eternity
of the human soul. He knows very well that man
is a fruit that is still unripe, hard, green and
sour. So, just as he ripens fruit on trees, filling
them little by little with sugar until they have a
delicious flavour, he also ripens humanity. But
he has also understood that humans take longer
to reach maturity than fruit and trees, so he has
decided to be patient. He knows that if he continues to warm even a criminal, that criminal
will end by being so disgusted with himself that
he will accept the sun's influence and change
into something absolutely adorable: a sensitive
poet, a musician, a benefactor of mankind!
The sun never abandons men because he
knows that if he did their evolution would mis-
carry: there would be no more ripe fruit, no

more saints or prophets, no more divinities on earth. The sun continues to warm and give light to men because he knows the causes and the consequences of their evolution, the beginning and the end, as well as the path they have to tread. If he did not know all this, he would be furious, he would close up and become dark and that would be the end of mankind! The fact that the sun goes on shining is proof that he knows the purpose of his work, the goal of creation, and he continues to help humanity to reach maturity.

To the sun we are like seeds planted in spiritual soil: if we benefit from his rays we are capable of producing flowers with such marvellous scents that even divinities will be in raptures over them. What is a flower? It cannot sing, nor dance, nor play the violin, and yet singers, dancers and musicians marvel at it. And we, if we learn to be like flowers, why should we not attract divinities that are so far above us? They will cluster round in raptures over us, exclaiming, 'Oh, what lovely flowers!' And they will care for us and help us to become even more pure and luminous and fragrant.

There! The sun knows all that and that is why he, alone, never tires of doing good to human beings. Everyone else gets tired. They close shop and vanish from the scene: dead and gone!

But the sun is always there, triumphant and radiant. He says, 'Come and quench your thirst, take from me. Have you done something wrong? I shan't hold it against you. Human beings are selfish, evil and vindictive and if you fall into their hands there's no knowing where you'll end. But I'm not like them. I shan't harm you. Come. Open yourself to my rays. I can give you so much!' So if we take the sun as our ideal and our model we can become better human beings. When we are near him we find the courage to forget all the difficulties and disappointments that we have met with amongst our fellow humans. If we learn to think like the sun we can become divinities for we shall never lose patience. Everyone else is defeated after a while and tells you, 'Go away. I don't want to see you anymore. I've done all I can for you and now I'm tired. Go on, get out!' But the sun never tires of us. Now, perhaps, you understand why I want to lead you to the sun: because he, and only he, can inspire you with noble, divine sentiments.

One day, with the idea of getting to know the sun's philosophy better, I made an appointment with him! Yes! We met in a pub, and after ordering our drinks, I said to him, 'My dear sun, tell me. There's something that is not quite clear to me: how is it that you shine so brightly?' And do you know what he told me? He said, 'It's because I'm burning with love and love produces light.' Then I asked, 'But please explain to me how you can go on and on loving human beings and giving them your light when you know better than anyone how wicked they are.' And the sun replied, 'Oh, you know, I decided a long time ago not to bother about what they were like. I only look after myself, and since it gives me so much pleasure to spread the warmth of my love all around me, I go on doing it and I'm always happy. As to whether humans appreciate me or not, that's all the same to me, and I advise you to be like me. If you begin to worry about their reactions you won't be able to bear it.'

So, I decided to imitate the sun, and that is why I can go on with my work. For, if you believe that humans appreciate me and want to help me, you are mistaken! I'm a thorn in the side of many and they would dearly love to be rid of me! I assure you: when I see how deceitful, spiteful, self-seeking and ungrateful some are, I feel like packing my bags and leaving people to their own devices. Fortunately the sun is there, and he whispers, 'Remember our conversation in the pub.' 'Ah, yes, yes', I reply, and go on with my work. And now what about you? Why shouldn't you imitate the sun, too?

It appears that science has already calculated the date of the sun's death, in fact some American scientists believe that he is already very ill! But the truth is that the sun possesses the secret of prolonging his own life for as long as he wants, until his whole family has reached perfection. You see, he does have a family to bring up and to provide for. All the planets which gravitate around him are his children and he cannot die until they have reached perfection, that is, until they too have become suns, like their father.

9

THE TRUE SOLAR RELIGION

I

Light, warmth and life! The light, the warmth and the life that flow so ceaselessly and in such abundance from the sun! We still have not exhausted all that is contained in these three notions. And now I want to show you how that light, warmth and life can help us to understand one of the most obscure tenets of the Christian religion: the Holy Trinity.

Theologians tell us that the Trinity is a mystery: the mystery of one God in three persons. But what can human beings do with a mystery? They just leave it alone and forget about it. Whereas we on the contrary, encounter the Holy Trinity every day, we salute it, spend time in its presence and rejoice in our contemplation of it. The Church may well say that this is blasphemy. Perhaps! But if you talk to human beings about a Divinity that is so abstract and distant you must not be surprised at the results: they will no longer have any feeling for the Divine Being. He will no longer dwell in them and they will have no reason to prevent themselves from giving way to their worst instincts and committing every senseless and immoral act that comes into their heads.

In the new religion that is coming nearer and nearer, and which will, one day, embrace the whole world, spiritual realities will be closer and more accessible and people will be able to live them and feel them, to communicate and unite with them. Every day they will receive such an extraordinarily luminous nourishment that they will be obliged to transform themselves. For, only if he absorbs the best possible nourishment on all levels, can man really be transformed.

Under different names, the Trinity can be found in all the religions of the world. There is always the notion of one original Being who engenders another who, in turn, engenders a third. In Christianity they are called Father, Son and Holy Spirit. The Father is the Life that floods the whole universe, the fountain-head of all creation. The Son might be called the Light, for Christ said, 'I am the Light of the world.' But he is also Love, that is: warmth. And the Holy Spirit is sometimes identified with Love and sometimes with the Light that illuminates men's intelligence and gives them the power to prophesy, to speak in tongues and to penetrate the great mysteries. In point of fact it makes no difference which Person of the Trinity is seen as Love and which one is seen as Light. The Son and the Holy Spirit are one, they each become the other, they both have the same powers.

What is essential is to understand that these three principles, Father, Son and Holy Spirit, are present in the life, the light and the warmth of the sun. The Father is Life; the Son is Love or Light and the Holy Spirit is Light or Love. You may ask, 'But do we have the right to see such exalted Beings in the light, warmth and life of the sun?' Yes, indeed you do. And this correspondence is of great practical value: it means that we can contemplate the Holy Trinity every single day. It means that we can enter into communion and form a bond with the Trinity and benefit from all its great blessings. It is a promise of resurrection and life.

Why cannot Christians understand that the greatest truths are all there, before them, visible to the naked eye? Before long everyone will have understood except Christians! They will still be saying, 'Oh, you know, it's not the sun that matters. Even if the sun didn't exist, what would still matter would be the Mass. It's the Mass that will save us.' They have never realized that if the sun did not exist no one would be alive to say Mass. They themselves would have been dead, frozen,

turned to stone, ages ago. Christians beat everyone else for blindness and narrow-mindedness! I
can hear you protesting, 'But what have you got
against Christians?' Nothing! Nothing at all! I
am a Christian too. If I shake them up a bit from
time to time, it is simply to try to get them to
open their eyes and see things a little more
clearly.

When the world above created the world below, it left signs, traces or reflections of itself so
that humans could follow these signs and make
their way to it. And one of these reflections is
the sun. The Trinity has no wish to remain forever hidden and inaccessible to human beings:
It manifests Itself to them by means of the sun so
that they can find their way to It. This is something we have to be clear about: the Holy Trinity is not actually contained in the light, warmth
or life of the sun. It is infinitely, unutterably
greater. But we can use that light, warmth and
life as a means of access to the Trinity, as a way
of entering into a communion of love with it, as
a channel through which we can call upon it to
penetrate our whole being.

And, since we are created in the image of
God, each one of us must be a trinity. In fact,
thanks to our three faculties of intellect, heart
and will, we are already a trinity: a trinity which
thinks, feels and acts. But, of course, this little

trinity is completely lacking in light, life or warmth. It needs to be reanimated, warmed and illuminated by the sun. So, here again, we see the use of being present at the sunrise: little by little our own tiny trinity becomes luminous, warm and vital, like the sun. It begins to draw a little nearer to the great Trinity of Father, Son and Holy Spirit.

Christ said, 'Be ye perfect as your Heavenly Father is perfect.' But, as we have never seen the Father, where can we find a model of His perfection? Here, in the sun, we have the model we need. God is very far above us, very, very far away, but in His mercy He has given men the means to find Him. He has, as it were, blazed the trail, and if we follow that trail which takes us through the sun, we will reach the Father.

Every day, we have before our eyes a sublime image of the Holy Trinity, and if we can learn to work with this image, our own little trinity will become holy. Everybody repeats Christ's words, 'Be ye perfect as your Heavenly Father is perfect,' but as long as we do not know how the Father manifests Himself, if we have no notion or perception of His vibrations, His colours, His power, then Christ's injunction remains purely theoretical. The sun can explain to us that the Father, the Son and the Holy Spirit are indissolubly one. In the minds of many Christians, the three Persons of the Trinity are separate and distinct, but in reality they are one : three in one. In the Cabbalah One is Three and Three is One.

In man, similarly, the intellect, heart and will are never separate. They are welded together and they work and advance all together. The intellect formulates its plans and the heart encourages it, 'Go on, go on! I'm with you.' And the will hastens to carry out the plans. All three gallop abreast to put an idea into effect. Sometimes, however, one can see that it is the will that rushes ahead of the mind and the heart. And if the intellect lags too far behind disaster follows. Even if it shouts after the will, 'Wait for me. Don't go so fast. You're making a mistake!' the will just answers, 'Shut up. You don't know what you're talking about!' Oh, yes. The three of them have some great discussions... but it is not yet a holy trinity !

If we want our own little trinity to be holy we have to adopt the sun as our model and strive to resemble him more and more in order to become luminous, warm-hearted and vibrant with life as he is. Of course, it is not possible to attain the fullness of perfection manifested by the sun, but the work we put into it is in the direct line of Initiation. Instead of being bogged down in old, useless, outdated notions, it is far better to go and contemplate the sun and strive to reach the ideal of becoming like him. As I have already told you, there is a law of mimicry, according to which all creatures end by resembling their own environment. If a person often spends time, a lot of time, contemplating the sun, if he loves and understands the sun and soaks up his light with all his being, gradually he will become like him. And if he knows how to collect and condense the sun's rays and store them up in his solar plexus, he will have the power to draw on his reserves when he needs to and, in this way, he will become tireless. This is a profound science which has to be studied, a real training programme which requires serious work, and those who do take it seriously will be astonished to see how, every day of their lives, their efforts will be abundantly rewarded.

How is it possible that people do not realize that it is the sun who manifests most adequately the generosity, the immensity and the eternity of God? If we want to seek the Holy Trinity we must turn to the sun. Every teacher knows that you have to begin by showing children the concrete, tangible aspects of things first, that which can be seen and touched, before trying to teach them more abstract things. Religion should have been taught in the same way. Instead of speaking of the Divinity, of the Holy Trinity in such abstract terms that no one, or practically no one, can understand the first thing about it, it would have been so much better to begin with something more concrete and accessible : the sun. We should begin by putting ourselves in the presence of the sun, by drinking in his warmth, light and love, and by thanking God for them. After that, if we have the mental capacity to do so, we can go further and seek the Cosmic Spirit, the Absolute.

Perhaps you will ask, 'But can't we find God in church, in the Sacred Host?' And the answer, of course, is : yes, you can find God in church. But what church, what temple could possibly be compared to Nature? And what host could be compared to the sun? You can eat wagon-loads of hosts and still be just as evil, jealous, sensual, stupid and sickly as you were before. Whereas if you go to the sun, that immense host, and if you partake of it every day, you will be obliged to transform yourself. For nowhere else does God manifest Himself in all His power, light and warmth as potently as He does in the sun.

Besides, if you think of it, who can deny that even the Host is made of materials supplied by the sun? And no one ever thinks of thanking the sun. We accept everything he has to offer : wheat and grapes, and we forget to say 'Thank you.' We do not even think that without the sun we could never make a single Host nor one drop of

Wine. Why have men been so misled? Why has the importance of the sun been hidden from them? Why have they been taught to believe that they will find God in the Bread and Wine? In truth it is possible to find God in these symbols, but only if one learns what the symbols really mean.

As you know, the origin of Holy Communion is the Last Supper that Jesus ate with his disciples. He took the bread and wine in his hands and said, 'Take, this is my body... Drink ye all of it, for this is my blood... Whoso eateth my flesh and drinketh my blood hath eternal life...' In point of fact, bread and wine were two deeply significant symbols which were known to men long before the time of Jesus.

If you read the Bible you will learn that Melchizedek was the first to institute the rite of Communion when he presented Abraham with the gift of bread and wine. Melchizedek was the King of Justice (in Hebrew, *Melek* means king and *Zedek* means justice), and he dwelt in the Kingdom of Salem (Salem has the same root as *Shalom*: peace). That is why Melchizedek is called the King of Justice and Peace. He brought the bread and wine to Abraham as a reward for his victory over the seven sinister kings of Edom, for those seven kings symbolized the Seven Deadly Sins. You must not think that Melchi-

zedek, the greatest of all Initiates, went out of his
way to reward Abraham for having killed a few
hundred, or even a few thousand, enemies in
battle. Abraham came from Ur in Chaldea (and
Ur means light). He practised magic and called
up spirits and it was on the advice of the spirits
who were at his service that he went to Egypt to
complete his initiation. So Melchizedek gave
Abraham the bread and wine, and one might be
tempted to think that this was not much of a reward, unless, of course, one understands their
symbolic value. In reality, bread and wine represent the whole of Initiatic Science which is based
on the two cosmic principles: the masculine
principle, symbolized by the bread, and the feminine principle, symbolized by the wine, for
these two principles are at work in all regions of
the universe.

Bread and wine are solar symbols. It is not a
question of the physical reality of bread and
wine, but of the two properties of the sun: light
and heat, which combine together to create life.
But the heat is love, the light, wisdom. And so
we can see that Jesus meant that if we ate his
flesh, wisdom, and drank his blood, love, we
would have eternal life.

For two thousand years, now, Christians
have been eating wagon-loads of hosts and
drinking barrels of wine without ever attaining

everlasting life and even, sadly enough, without being in any way the better for it. The only way to attain eternal life is to eat the light and drink the warmth of Christ, the Spirit of the sun.

II

When Jesus said, 'No one can go to the Father except through me,' it was Christ who was speaking through him. He was saying, 'No one can go to the Father unless he goes through me because I am the Spirit of Christ who manifests Himself through the sun.' You may object that this is an arbitrary interpretation, but that is not so. I could show you how you can situate each truth in its right place. We find truths scattered and seemingly disconnected but an Initiate must find the links between them and fit each one into its rightful place in the great Living Book of Nature.

I have already shown you how, with his warmth and light and with the life he gives us, the sun is the most perfect image of the Trinity we could have here on this earth. The life that flows through the sun is the Father. The light and the warmth can be seen respectively, either as the Son or as the Holy Spirit, but for an Initiate, the Holy Spirit is best portrayed by warmth, that is, love, and the Son, Christ, is best portrayed by light, that is, wisdom.

The light that flows from the sun, therefore, that light that produces such tremendous transformations in the universe, that brings with it such great benefits for all creatures and whose true nature is still unknown, that light is Christ, the Spirit of Christ. The light of the sun is a living spirit and it is by way of this light that the Spirit of Christ is always with us, unfailingly present and active, forever at work. If this were not so how could we understand the words, 'I am the Light of the world,' or 'My Father and I are one'? They are one in the sun, for it is in the sun that light and life are one. And then again, Jesus said, 'I am the Resurrection and the Life.' Who raises the dead to life? Who gives us life? None other than Christ, the Spirit of Christ who dwells in the sun.

Christians have a tendency to see Christ in a particular place, usually, of course, in Palestine, since that is where Jesus lived. But if He is truly the Resurrection and the Life, He dwells not in Palestine but in the sun. Of course, Christ is everywhere in Nature, but as far as we are concerned He is in the sun. And that is why, if you can get into the habit of contemplating the sun in the morning, remembering that it is Christ who is there before your eyes, and if you link with Him and love Him, your whole being will throb and vibrate in harmony with the Cosmic Light that shines, in condensed form, through the sun.

Of course, Christ is far greater than the sun. He is the Son of God, the Second Person of the Trinity, manifesting not through our sun alone, but through all the innumerable suns that exist in the cosmos, many of them far bigger and more brilliant than ours. This is why, when I talk of Christ, I am not talking about Jesus, but about the Cosmic Principle that knows no beginning and no end. Jesus was a man who lived in Palestine two thousand years ago, who was so pure, so noble and so highly evolved that when he was thirty years old he received the Holy Spirit and, at the same time, the Spirit of Christ. That is why he is called Jesus-Christ. But Christ can be born in the hearts and souls of all human beings. It was Christ who manifested himself in Orpheus, Moses, Zarathustra, Buddha and all the great Initiates of all lands and all ages.

There is only one Jesus, but there are, or there can be, thousands of Christs. Jesus will always be a unique figure. He is the head of the Christian religion, just as Buddha is the head of Buddhism and Mohammed the head of the Moslem religion. But Christ is the head of the whole of humanity, even of the whole universe: not the head of one religion, but of all religions. It was Christ who inspired religion. And this is why men must get rid of all racial or sectarian overtones in their religions. Even Christianity is still a sectarian religion. In the Old Testament God was the God of the Israelites alone. They were the only ones who had the right to survive, the right to dominate and even massacre other peoples. Later on, Christians used the New Testament in the same way, with the idea that they alone were chosen and beloved, the Lord's elect, and all others were infidels. Here you have the Christians' greatest mistake: just as the sun shines for all men without discrimination, in the same way the Lord loves all His children. If this were not so we would have to conclude that the sun was more loving and more generous than God Himself!

How can one get human beings to realize how ridiculous it is to try to win God over to their side? Look at what goes on when two countries go to war: with pomp and ceremony the priests bless their respective armies and weaponry, imploring God to give them victory and wipe out their enemies. They even try to gain His favours with offerings of hymns, prayers and incense! What a deplorable mentality! We must never try to bribe God. From an ordinary human standpoint, of course all this is quite normal. Everyone tries to protect his own interests. But if you rise above this level to a higher level you will see that, just like the sun, God is absolutely impartial and even leaves men free to massacre each other, since that seems to be what they enjoy most!

One of the essential aspects of a solar philosophy is that it leads to a spirit of universality. We have to cease wanting one race or another, one people or another, one supreme religion or ideology to dominate the whole world. All men must advance together towards the only universal religion, that of Love.

Believe me, the Lord is like the sun : different races, religions and ideologies leave Him completely indifferent. It simply does not bother Him whether you are yellow, black or red, whether you are a Jew, a Catholic, a Protestant or even an atheist. We are all His children and He cares only about our qualities and virtues : our love, wisdom, honesty and generosity.

Always keep in your mind's eye this image of the sun as the most perfect representative of the Divinity. How is it that people who find it normal to go to their church or temple and bow or kneel in prayer before an icon or the statue of a saint, think it quite abnormal to contemplate the sun? Why do they imagine that they will get more light and comfort from praying in front of something made by human beings who were not always especially pure or honourable, than they would get from praying before the sun who comes, bursting with life straight from the hand of God? Go to church or to the temple if you want to, I sometimes do so myself, but know that only the sun will teach you to live the divine life.

By the same author:
(translated from the French)

Izvor Collection

The Complete Works of Omraam Mikhaël Aïvanhov
Original Edition in French

EDITOR – DISTRIBUTOR

FRANCE   Editions PROSVETA S.A. – B.P. 12
83601 Fréjus Cedex

DISTRIBUTORS

BRITISH ISLES PROSVETA Ltd. – The Doves Nest,
Duddleswell,
Uckfield, East Sussex T N 22 3JJ
Trade orders to :
ELEMENT Books Ltd
Unit 25 Longmead Shaftesbury
Dorset SP7 8PL

CANADA   PROSVETA Inc. – 1565 Montée Masson
Duvernay est, Laval, Qué. H7E 4P2

DENMARK   SANKT ANSGARS FORLAG
Bredgade 67 – 1260 Copenhague

HOLLAND   UITGEVERIJ SERVIRE B.V.
Varkevisserstraat 52
NL – 2225 Katwij aan Zee

HONG KONG HELIOS
31 New Kap Bin Long Village
Sai Kung N.T., Hong Kong

IRELAND   PROSVETA IRL.
84 Irishtown – Clonmel

NORWAY   PROSVETA NORGE
Husebyveien 8b
0379 Oslo 3

UNITED STATES PROSVETA U.S.A. – P.O. Box 49614
Los Angeles, California 90049